Home is where the things that happen in this book happen. They happen to happen to Cynthia Lindsay because it's <u>her</u> home. And there's no place like it.

Why?

Because Cynthia Lindsay has a greater genius than any other living homester for nonstop, nonpareil confusion. Pay close attention to what she has to <u>say</u>; just don't do what she's done.

Do you have:

garden problems? In "The Case of the Black Thumb," Mrs. L shows you how to let your garden cultivate you.

décor problems? Here's how to match a goldfish.

portage problems? Banish them. Learn how to pack a gondola.

lobster problems? Study "Crustaceans Anonymous or How to Sober Up a Lobster."

HOME

IS WHERE

YOU HANG

YOURSELF

or

How to Be a Woman -
and Who Needs It?

BY

CYNTHIA LINDSAY

Simon and Schuster · New York · 1962

SECOND PRINTING

*Grateful acknowledgment is made to the follow-
ing magazines for permission to include selections that originally appeared in their pages:*

Vogue: "The Occupation" and "My Life on
the Creamed-Chicken Circuit."
McCall's Magazine: "Thirteen Safe Rules on
What Absolutely Never, Ever to Say to Your
Husband Under Any Circumstances."
Harper's Bazaar: "The Confessions of a Pack
Rat."
Show Business Illustrated: "The Goose
Route."

LIBRARY OF CONGRESS CATALOG CARD NUMBER: 62-7554
MANUFACTURED IN THE UNITED STATES OF AMERICA
BY VAIL-BALLOU PRESS, INC., BINGHAMTON, N.Y.

To my husband,
with love . . .

The art of being a woman successfully can be learned neither from life nor from a charm school. It is a quality mysteriously endowed at birth—a magic quality. If it is inherent in you, you are blessed indeed. If it isn't, you just have to keep trying—harder, and harder— and harder.

Plan your life, organize your time, and if you can't learn from your own experiences, try to learn from those of others—mine, for instance. There may be a little something useful you can pick up in this "How to" in Womanship; if so, I'm grateful that I've contributed to easing your situation while complicating my own.

But as you go on your womanly way, remember, and keep always in mind, the one imperative fact: You Can't Win.

CONTENTS

9

CONTENTS

THE

OCCUPATION

or

How

to Be a

Breadwinner

F OR RENT: GUESTHOUSE. Tenant must be fond of children and dogs."

It seemed like a good idea at the time: I was a widow with a small boy and had listened carefully to lectures about a woman alone needing income property. So I built this little house at the back of the garden and furnished it so attractively that I momentarily considered just keeping it as a guesthouse, except that it was now going to be essential to get the income from it to make up, at least in part, for the outgo on it.

When the doorbell rang, in answer to my ad, and I viewed my first possible tenant, every instinct cried out *"No."* But who listened?

"Please come in," I said to a mournful, gray-haired woman with heavy dewlaps and moist, reproachful eyes.

She flumped into a chair and mopped her forehead with a flowered handkerchief. "I wonder if I could trouble you for a glass of water?" She sighed. "You have quite a walk here from the bus stop, you know."

Good! Encouraged by her complaining tone, I brought her the water and said, "I guess you'd find us too far from transportation for your convenience."

"Well," she said, "we all have to put up with things we don't like in order to gain something we do. I like your attitude about children and dogs."

"It's a necessary one," I replied. "I have a small son and two very noisy poodles, so anyone renting the guesthouse would be subjected to a certain amount of both."

"Oh, I wouldn't mind at all," she said, and I began to feel more apprehensive. "Maybe I'd better tell you a little about myself," she added, sinking deeper into the chair.

Between sighs and rushing of tears to the eyes, I learned she was a flower painter—she painted pictures of them, not the flowers. She also painted pictures of dogs and children, from snapshots. She also painted nylon underwear. In this case she painted the underwear, not pictures of it. Garlands of flowers, little sayings, hearts, and that sort of thing. This she did at night. During the day she worked in a gift shop. She was quiet; she loved children—and animals. And speaking of animals—and then the tears overflowed: "I have a very old dog. No one will rent to me because they don't want him. If you'll take us in, I'll do anything—sit with your little boy evenings—anything." She had me. Aside from being disastrously fond of animals, I was suffering from a bad case of cabin fever and the thought of some free evenings clinched the deal. Miss Gunter moved in that night. My son Michael and I were introduced to Gordon.

Gordon was as old and unattractive a semi-collie as I'd ever seen. I looked in dismay at the clouds of loose hair that blew from him like snow from a mountaintop.

As Michael and I helped her in with what appeared to be an endless series of boxes, paper bags, and pictures, I came to a few conclusions: that Miss Gunter was a very bad painter, that she was a mystic—there were reams of pamphlets on self-help, occult healing, and transcendentalism—that she did something peculiar with purple velvet—there was a great deal of it—and that this whole thing wasn't going to work out. I was 100 per cent right all around, although I never really found out about the velvet.

The first few days were uneventful. I was busy, kept away from the guesthouse, and it didn't occur to me to wonder what Gordon did with his time while his mistress was at work. I found out only by accident.

Miss Gunter requested more blankets and I took them out to the house. The sight that met my startled eyes made it all too plain how Gordon occupied himself all day: he ate mattresses. He also ate chair seats and the edges of curtains. Whether from hunger or ennui, Gordon had a preoccupation with kapok.

The house was full of it. Gordon thumped his thin, hairy tail in greeting as I entered, and Miss Gunter smiled her rigor-mortis smile at me.

"Don't worry about the untidiness," she said. Untidiness! "I'll fix it," she went on. "That's why I wanted the blankets. I can put them over that place in the mattress."

"That place" was a gaping hole approximately three by four feet in the center of the bed.

"I'll have it fixed next week, as soon as I get some money," she added.

I was too staggered to make any comment on the condition of the house, but the word "money" helped to make me more articulate. "Well, as long as you have it fixed—" I said weakly. "But speaking of money—"

"I know," she said. "The rent. I'm sorry I haven't done anything about it yet—I'm a little short—but I have a proposition for you. I get a hundred dollars for a portrait. I'll paint yours, life-size, for the fifty I owe you. It really is a bargain."

"Miss Gunter," I said, picking pieces of kapok off

my dress, "I need a life-sized portrait of myself as much as I need a third elbow. I'm sorry." I walked out, suspecting she was crying, but telling myself I *must* be tough.

For the next few days Miss Gunter avoided me. If I approached her she bit her lower lip, puddled up, and looked away. Then one night she appeared at the back door, misty-eyed and reproachful in manner. She handed me some money. "I'm very sorry I couldn't give you this before," she said, "but we had to eat, too, you know."

The implication that I was snatching the food from Gordon's jowls irritated me. I would have thought Gordon so full of kapok there wouldn't be room for anything else. I thanked her, and she handed me a bunch of dreadful crocheted flowers. "I thought you might like these to wear to a party. I made them myself."

This "returning good for evil" technique was lost on me. I said to myself, Be tough, mention the fact that the rent was three weeks overdue. To her I just said, "Thank you so much. How's Gordon?"

"Oh, he is as well as can be expected," she answered mournfully. "He's very old, you know. We're both very, very old."

This really wasn't my fault. The attitude of general reproach was beginning to be annoying. "I do hope," I said, trying to sound like a landlady, "that Gordon hasn't destroyed any more furniture."

"No," she replied. "He's much less restless now. You see, I leave the lights on, keep the stove going for warmth, and the radio playing all day while I'm gone—the music station, you know, it seems to soothe him. Well, good night."

"Good night," I said.

My God! Lights, gas, radio—all day, every day. Measures must be taken.

The following evening, with trepidation, I knocked on her door.

"Yes?" she said. Obviously I was intruding.

"May I talk to you for a moment?" I said. "Or am I disturbing your dinner?"

"Well, I was just getting a bite . . ." She nodded toward the table. Even the tongue on the plate seemed to be going "Tsk, tsk, tsk."

And then I knew we were not alone. I felt a riveting gaze and looked up into the slightly crossed eyes of the most enormous, and certainly the ugliest, cat I had ever seen, lying on top of the dresser, its head resting on a pink satin pincushion. It was a no-color cat, or rather an all-color cat—mostly orange.

"This," she said, "is Deirdre."

"Hello, Deirdre," I said.

Deirdre stared malevolently at me.

"I know I should have told you about her," Miss Gunter fluttered. "She belonged to a friend of mine—a spiritualist—she just passed beyond. I felt that Deirdre needed me. She's very good company for Gordon.

I knew you'd understand." She coughed feebly. Gordon scratched his ear, very slowly, and Deirdre yawned. Some of her teeth were missing. I understood perfectly: Miss Gunter was a witch and Gordon and Deirdre her familiars. My courage fled and so did I.

"Well, good night," I said, heading for the door.

"But you wanted to talk to me—"

"It can keep," I said.

Another period of no contact ensued. The time for the rent arrived and passed. I was gathering my strength to give Miss Gunter notice when Deirdre precipitated the action.

I was walking across the garden and stopped to listen to the series of sounds emanating from the guesthouse. There was a scratching, tearing noise, low growling, and feline howls, all of which *segued* into the "William Tell Overture" from the radio. I knew my tenant not only drew the blinds but also locked the door, and was wondering whether I could get in through a window when Deirdre saved me the trouble by coming out through one, followed closely by Gordon, showing enormous vitality for a dog of his age. They tore across the yard and I climbed through the window.

The sight that met my eyes was staggering. Miss Gunter apparently shared her rooms with poltergeists as well as familiars. All of the stuffing was out of *everything;* the place was covered as from a landslide in cotton and kapok. The refrigerator door was lying on the floor. The mirrors above the bar were broken in two, and above them was a series of small round spots, the kind I hadn't seen since at boarding school we used to throw butter balls at the ceiling. Possibly this was how Miss G. entertained her friends.

The worst damage was to the wallpaper. It had been very nice wallpaper, but Deirdre had taken care of that. She had put those stubby little claws in and ripped off sheet after sheet. As I stood transfixed in the wreckage, the door opened and Miss Gunter entered, followed by Michael.

He said, "Gee—gosh!"

She said, "Oh dear—where are they?"

I said, "I don't know where they *are,* but I know where they aren't *going* to be. I am very sorry, but I must ask you to leave as soon as possible, Miss Gunter. I am giving you notice now."

Miss Gunter's eyes moistened and she started to speak, but as she did so, the strangest noise yet came from under her bed, providing an exotic counterpoint to the William Tell. It was a dry, clicking, parchment-like sound, coming with great regularity. Click, scrape, click, scrape.

"What's *that?*" I gasped.

"Hey, Mom, look!" said Michael, and pointed to the bed. From under it emerged the head of a giant land tortoise—it looked steadily at us and came the rest of the way out. Over the tortoise's shell was a pink baby blanket printed with little white bunnies. The edge of the blanket was tied under its chin with pink ribbon, and the remainder covered its three-foot length like a cape.

"That's Pandora," said Miss Gunter. "I didn't tell you about her because she only gets up on the fifteenth of April. She sleeps the rest of the year, so I knew she wouldn't be any trouble. She's three hundred years old and very quiet really."

I was speechless, but my son wasn't. He was overcome with delight. "Three hundred years old! Golly, Mom, that's older than you are!"

Slowly, steadily, and rather regally, with her blanket dragging, Pandora was making for the door.

"Would you excuse me a minute?" said Miss Gunter. "She's always terribly thirsty when she wakes up, and I don't like to keep her waiting. A year's a long time to go without a drink."

I agreed, thinking I could use one myself.

My son was trailing Pandora. "May I take her blanket off, Miss Gunter?"

"Yes, Michael, but carefully—so as not to startle her. She's still a little sleepy."

Pandora looked pretty alert to me and was moving relentlessly to the door. Michael, Miss Gunter, and I followed her outside to the dog's water bowl. "She'll drink for twenty minutes, if you have something else to do," said Miss Gunter.

Pandora did—exactly twenty minutes by my watch. Miss Gunter went off and returned with Deirdre and

Gordon. Gordon looked tired, Deirdre triumphant. Miss Gunter said, "She's through now. Michael, would you be kind enough to pick some roses? All she eats are the petals."

Michael was happy to comply and returned with a handful of my best. It was too late; I was in this too deep. As I saw the first rose (Mrs. Calvin Coolidge, if I remember rightly) go down, I bowed to defeat. On completion of her meal, Pandora raised her head, looked me full in the eye, and belched—very loudly.

"Isn't she *wonderful?*" shouted my son.

"Just wonderful," I said weakly and went into the house and made a double martini.

My son joined me, with an apple juice on the rocks. "Miss Gunter says that I can help take care of Pandora," he said. "She's gone back to bed now. I put her blanket back on. But every April fifteenth I can get her up and feed her. Isn't that *great?*"

"Just great," I replied.

That night, after I had sunk into a troubled sleep, I was wakened by the noise of the garden gate stealthily opening. Looking out the window, I could see a figure carrying boxes. The figure slipped through the gate, closely followed by two furry shapes. Miss Gunter and her familiars were running out on the rent. I tiptoed downstairs and locked up our dogs so they wouldn't bark.

THE POSTMAN

RINGS

CONSTANTLY

or

How

to Become Involved

in a Mail Robbery

I GOT OFF to a bad start with Mr. Mason, the postman at our new old house. Not bad from a human-relations standpoint—we quite liked each other. It was just that he thought me peculiar. There was some justification for this opinion.

Two young girl students from the university nearby had joined Michael and me as paying guests. The girls hadn't read as many "before and after" pieces in home magazines as I, but they were quite stimulated about remodeling. Mike had never been as happy and as unrepressed as when allowed to spend his time helping to knock down walls. As I was doing most of the remodeling myself, I was generally garbed in blue jeans and T shirt.

Mr. Mason's first day at our house, I was so garbed. I charged out the front door full of enthusiasm and covered with plaster, a broom in one hand and a sack of old wallpaper in the other. One of the students was chopping down the jungle of weeds which comprised our front lawn. I beamed at her, raised a clenched fist, and cried, "Fight on, Comrade." Mr. Mason looked steadily from one of us to the other. I had to be funny— I wasn't aware that the people from whom I had purchased the house had left the country after being investigated by the House Un-American Activities Committee. Mr. Mason apparently was.

As no copies of the *People's World* appeared in the mail for me, and as I began to be seen occasionally with a clean face and a dress, I think his suspicions on this score were abated if not eliminated entirely. They were, however, rapidly replaced by others.

As the period of reconstruction wore on, Mr. Mason began to take an interest in the external structural changes. The house was an old square frame building which looked as if the top of it had been neatly sliced off by a giant knife. It had a definitely New England feeling about it as it stood high above the Spanish bungalows on the street, so I had a widow's walk built on the roof. It looked fine, and I was standing on the sidewalk admiring it when Mr. Mason arrived. He stood beside me for a moment, then said, "You think it's safe?"

"What?" I said.

"The playpen up there on the roof," he said. "Seems a funny place to put one."

"It's a widow's walk, Mr. Mason," I replied.

He cast his eyes down respectfully. "Oh, I'm sorry— excuse me," he said.

He apparently thought he had said the wrong thing. I hastened to put him at ease. "It's not practical, Mr. Mason," I said, "just decoration. The real ones served a purpose. The wives of New England fishermen used to stand on their roof tops and wait for their husbands' ships to come in. Sometimes they never came—that's why they're called widow's walks."

"No kiddin'?" he said. "Well, if you ain't gonta use it, what you got it up there for?"

Without waiting for an answer, he looked toward the garage and frowned. "And what the hell is that on the roof?" he said. "Looks just like a doghouse."

"It is," I said. "For bird dogs." I chuckled slightly at my own joke.

Mr. Mason was looking at me as if hoping his worst fears would not be realized.

"You see," I said defensively, "I hated the shape of the garage. The former owners left a doghouse here, so I put it on the roof. When it's painted and has a weather vane on it, the whole building will look like a barn."

He studied it. "Yeah, I guess it will," he said. "Is that good?"

"I like it," I replied. "It's all a matter of taste."

"Yeah," he said. "It sure takes all kinds." He looked at the doghouse again, shook his head, and moved off.

The day the house was painted charcoal black with a white trim his attitude was more one of anger than of wonderment. I was outside, looking proudly at the effect of the first coat of paint, when the mail arrived. As usual, Mr. Mason stood silently beside me for a moment, looking. "That black stuff to keep the termites out?" he said.

"No," I replied. "That's the color it's being painted."

"Black?" he croaked.

"Well, it isn't exactly black. It's charcoal," I said weakly. He had me on the permanent defensive by this time.

"It's black," he said. "Is it cheaper than real paint?"

"No," I answered, "it's more expensive—and it *is* real paint."

He moved off but turned and said over his shoulder, "I'll say one thing for it. If you put satin curtains in the window, it'll look just like a great big coffin."

Mr. Mason had hurt my feelings, and it may have been partially to spite him that I allowed my son to carry through a household project he had in mind. He painted a horse's head looking out of the barn window. Mr. Mason didn't speak to me for a week.

In a short period of time I had established myself in Mr. Mason's mind as a possible Red and a definite mental case. It was no trouble at all convincing him that I was also an alcoholic. As the construction went on in the house, a great deal of loose lumber was left on the ground under the first floor. I was warned that this was meat for termites and should be removed. Having become dependent on child labor while reconstruction went on, I called Michael, told him to assemble his gang and some money might be made. Seven small boys arrived and I sent them under the house with a promised reward of a quarter apiece for bringing out the loose wood.

The morning of this activity, one of our college girls had put a Mexican piggy bank on the kitchen table and said, "This is almost full. When it is, the cocktails are on me. I've had too many of yours."

I mumbled something about "Oh, not at all, but that's very cute of you," and forgot all about it. Michael apparently didn't.

As the tribe of boys stood in a grubby line to be paid off, Mr. Mason arrived with the mail. He watched the group with interest.

"Here's yours, Chuck," I said. "And yours, Tony. And yours, Larry. Thank you, Jerry—and here, Bob." My son was next in line. "Here you are, Mike," I said.

"Don't bother about me, Mom," he said magnanimously. "Keep it and put it in the gin bank."

The kindness of one of my college girls put me back

on a talking basis with Mr. Mason. She was a French Canadian, and knowing that I had a passion for a Canadian cheese called Oka, she arranged for her parents to send me a box once a month. This necessitated constant negotiations between Mr. Mason and me because I invariably forgot there was a fifteen-cent duty to be paid on the package, and we would stand, the package between us, while he dug in his pockets to make change. Oka cheese shares one quality with limburger: it smells the same, only more so. The aroma permeates tin foil, wax paper, and outer wrapping alike and hangs, like a balloon, in the air. There was no indication on the outside what these packages contained. The wrapper simply read: "Les Pères Trappistes. La Trappe, Quebec."

One morning Mr. Mason arrived holding a Canadian package at arm's length. "Good morning, Mr. Mason," I said. "Aren't you awfully early?"

"Yeah," he said. "But they won't keep this down at the post office any longer. The postmaster says it's either him or it."

"I know it's hard to believe, Mr. Mason," I said, "but it tastes wonderful. I really believe it's one of the world's great cheeses."

His entire face brightened, "Oh, it's *cheese!*" he said. I never had the courage to ask him what he *thought* it was.

Some time later I was notified by a friend of the death of her husband. I felt the loss deeply and personally. He was a talented man, a fine writer, and I was sitting in my living room, thinking about the loss to literature as well as to his associates, when Michael came in. My friend and my son had been fond of each other. The adult had treated the child as an equal, and the small one had returned the compliment. Michael stood now, lanky in his blue jeans, idly aiming an empty slingshot at various pieces of bric-a-brac around the room. By his silent and almost courteous aspect it was obvious that he was going to ask a favor.

"Mike," I said, "I've got something to tell you. Sit down." He sat and leveled on me the embarrassed stare of the young when faced with seriousness in an elder. "Darling," I said, "Ann Saunders just called. John was very ill yesterday and died early this morning."

Michael showed no change of expression at first, then a look of disbelief crossed his face. "Oh no," he said. "He couldn't be—he was so much fun. Gosh, that's awful. What was the matter with him?"

"He had a heart attack. It was very quick—he was in no pain."

"Well, that's good," he said. Then he suddenly jumped up and said, "Say, Mom, Jay and I want to know if we can go to the show. There's two neat pictures at the El Miro. One about submarines and the other's all about a man who turns into a monster every time there's a full moon. Can we go?"

"By all means," I said coldly, horrified by the turning

off of grief and the switch to the desire for entertainment. I hoped and trusted that the chameleonlike change of emotion was normal. They can't, I thought, have a full realization of death at their age.

As I handed Mike and his weekend guest, Jay, the money for the show, I said, "Mike, it is customary to write a note to the husband or wife when someone dies, and I'd like you just to write Ann what you feel. I think it might make her happy to hear from you."

"Oh, sure," he said. They stamped out.

The boys returned from the movie enchanted by the degree of blood and gore to which they had been exposed, and with rousing appetites. After they had eaten steadily for what seemed to me an interminable length of time, I said, "I think now you had better get to that note."

Michael looked up with complete surprise and said, "What note?"

"The note to Ann about John—remember?"

"Oh, do I have to? We wanted to go across to Skip's. He's got a new sparrow hawk he just caught."

Jay then took up the chant. "Couldn't we, please? It's a real neat sparrow hawk—it can eat a whole lizard only swallowing once. I want to see it do it."

"Jay," I said, feeling my unpopularity mounting, "right now Michael has something to do, and he has to do it—*now*."

My son glared at me, threw his napkin down on the table, mumbled, "Oh, nuts," and the two boys stomped upstairs. I sat down with a book and tried to concentrate, but my head was full of thoughts of my friend and the future emptiness which faced his wife.

I turned some pages, but gradually the voices of the two boys upstairs intruded themselves:

"What do you suppose would happen if worlds did collide? If you were sitting up at the South Pole, for instance, would you still get squashed if the other world hit the North Pole first?"

"I guess you wouldn't know what hit you, anyway."

As I mounted the stairs the boys were discussing the relative merits of burying your enemy in sand up to his neck so the ants would eat him alive or hanging him from a tree for the vultures to get him. As I arrived at Michael's door they had switched to the latest moron joke.

"Why does the moron tiptoe by the medicine cabinet?"

"So he won't wake the sleeping pills," my son said as I entered.

"I don't like to interrupt," I said with sarcasm, "but I believe you were sent upstairs to write a letter. Now please go in the study and *write* it. Jay—you stay here until he finishes."

They looked at each other and shrugged with resignation. I returned to the living room and started again on the book. It hadn't been two minutes when a voice called down from the study:

"Mom—is this all right as a start? 'Dear Ann, I'm sorry John's dead . . .'"

"No, Mike, I don't think so. Ann is pretty upset, and that's a little shocking."

"Well, gosh, I don't know what to say . . ." He was starting to whine.

"Michael," I called back, "I am *not* going to dictate a letter. If it doesn't really come from you there is no point in writing it."

From upstairs came Jay's voice: "How about starting it this way—'Dear Ann, I'm sorry John kicked the bucket'?"

There was a shriek of laughter from Michael.

"Jay!" I shouted up the stairs. *"Please.* This is not something to joke about."

There was a complete silence except for the scratching of a pen for five minutes, then Michael bellowed, "Through! Come and look so we can get out of here!"

I went upstairs and on the desk in the study were two notes. Jay's recommendation: "Dear Ann, I'm sorry John kicked the bucket"—and the one Michael had just completed. The latter read: "Dear Ann, I felt very sorry when Mom told me about John. At first I couldn't believe it because he was so nice. And funny. I hope you are feeling well. Skip has a hawk, also an owl. I may get one. Or two. Love, Mike."

"That's a very nice note. Ann will love it," I said. "Now here's the address—stick it in an envelope, and you can run."

The following morning after breakfast the boys rose from the table and Michael said, "We're going to Skip's to watch the hawk eat the lizard."

"After you mail your letter, Mike. If you hurry, you can catch the postman. He's due now."

"Oh, Mom," he whinnied. "I'll be too late—he won't *eat* another one—oh, all right." He charged up the stairs four at a time and down five, raced for the front door, crashed into Mr. Mason, and said, "Oh—hi—here." He handed him the letter and ran up the street, followed by Jay.

Mr. Mason, catching his breath, said, "Growing fast, isn't he?"

"Too fast," I said. "Sorry about the collision." After a while I took the mail up to the study and sat down at my desk to open it. As I did so, a cold horror overtook me. On the desk was the *nice* letter to Ann Saunders.

I grabbed the phone, called the hawk-owning child's mother, and said rudely, "Send my son home *at once.*" I hung up and ran to the car. Michael and Jay met me there with startled faces, Michael with a young sparrow hawk on his wrist, and Jay with a huge, round-eyed barn owl on his shoulder. The additions to our group didn't help my mood.

"What's the matter, Mom?"

"The matter," I gasped to him, "is that you have just sent Ann the wrong letter!" I held out the nice letter. *"This* one you left on the desk."

"Oh no!" Michael said.

"Oh no," Jay repeated after him.

"Get in the car at once. We have to find Mr. Mason. You'll have to take those damned birds too—there's no time to return them!"

They piled in, birds and all, and I tore up the street.

Michael was genuinely alarmed. "What will Ann say? Will she be mad at me? Oh, Mom—you've got to find him!"

Jay also had the grace to feel guilty. "It's all my fault," he said, rather muffled through owl feathers.

For half an hour we drove around grimly. Michael was trying not to cry; Jay was silent. Only the birds were articulate. The hawk, unaccustomed to vehicular travel, was clinging to Michael's wrist, screaming, and beating its clipped wings, and the owl, opening and shutting its eyes, hissed rather like a serpent. It was a very tense carful when Michael suddenly shouted, "There he is!"

An overwhelming love for Mr. Mason flowed over me as I pulled over to the curb and we all leaped out. Mr. Mason looked startled, particularly at the sight of our feathered friends.

"Mr. Mason," I said, "it's too long a story—but you have a letter we must have back. It's addressed to Mrs. Ann Saunders, 471 Loma Terrace, Los Angeles. Please, would you look?"

He shifted his pack off his shoulder and looked at me sternly. "I can't do that—you should know better. It's against the law."

"But, Mr. Mason," I pleaded, "it's *our* letter."

"Not any more," he said, almost as if he were enjoying himself. "It belongs to good old Uncle Sam. Say, what are you doing with *them?*" The owl hissed and the hawk glared at him.

"Oh," I said frantically, "they just came along for the ride. Please, Mr. Mason, it's imperative we get the letter."

"Can't do it, ma'am—it's the *law*."

Then Michael saved the day by bursting into tears. "It's my letter," he sobbed. "I wrote it—can't you let us have it back if you see what's in it, so you know it isn't valuable or spy stuff or anything?"

Mr. Mason softened slightly. "Well, I suppose if you're willing to swear it's yours and identify the contents . . ."

"I'll swear anything," I said.

"Well—" he fumbled irritatingly through his bag— "I guess we can make an exception." After an interminable length of time he fished out our envelope and looked at it curiously. "Now," he said, "what does this important document say?"

"It says, 'Dear Ann, I'm sorry John kicked the bucket,'" I said.

He gave me *that* look again, then slowly opened the envelope, continuing to look searchingly at me over the top of it. We all, including the owl and the hawk, looked in. The envelope was absolutely empty.

I couldn't bear Mr. Mason's eyes so I turned on my son. *"Well?"* I said.

"Oh, golly," he said, "I just remembered, I stuck the letter in my pocket. I was going to put it in the envelope later, then you made me hurry so, I forgot and sent the envelope without it. I'm sorry, Mom." He reached in his pocket and withdrew the letter.

"This is the other letter," I said, handing it to the postman.

He read it, then slowly inserted it in the envelope he held. He licked the envelope. "Think that'll stick," he said. "That's O.K., son—we all make mistakes." He put the letter in his bag. "You know," he said, "that thing's kind of cute." He reached for the owl and it bit him.

Mr. Mason was transferred to another route that week, whether by due process, or at his own request, I don't know.

ROMANCE,

ROMANCE

or

How to Catch It—

Even

When You Don't Want It

THERE ARE WOMEN who draw romance to them as easily as they draw breath. Members of the opposite sex are attracted magnetically to them—a moth to a flame, a bee to a flower, a beatnik to a bongo. Specifically it is romantic dalliance we are discussing, not true love. A woman may have a True Love and also enjoy a spot of dalliance—it's the icing on top of the cake. It keeps her feeling female and desirable.

She may, for instance, flush with justifiable and not too guilty pleasure when dancing with an attractive stranger, as he brushes her hair gently with his lips, breathing into her ear, "What fragrance! You dance like an angel—a feather in my arms," and then, pressing her closer, says through just lightly clenched teeth, "I wonder what it would be like to *really* hold you in my arms!"

Now there is absolutely nothing the matter with that. He is never going to know what it's really like, because she is really a very good girl, faithful to the end to her True Love. However, for a few cherished moments, she feels a *femme fatale* incomparable, which is a good thing because her next dance is with her True Love, who brushes her hair out of his eye and breathes in her ear, "Who's leading, you or me?"

You, the woman, if you are a fortunate woman, may have innumerable little ego-inflaters in the form of these adventures. If you are romance-prone, voluntarily or involuntarily, something is going to happen—you can feel it in the air—it is like electricity.

I feel the electricity in the air, vibrate responsively to it, but something is wrong—the wires are crossed.

I think I must have a loose connection.

It isn't the time or the place that mainly appears to be at fault. It's the cast.

For instance, some years ago, before I was lucky enough to meet my True Love, I spent a couple of pleasant weeks in Cuba and Nassau. I was traveling with friends who were gay, good company. Cuba seemed to me a fairy-tale land where the sky and water competed for blueness, and where the fields were dotted with pink, blue, and yellow houses whose roofs were covered by a plant called Golden Rain; where the president lived in a marble palace, and the senators spoke of going into exile as one speaks of going away for a weekend: "Charming place, Miami. I spent my 1948 exile there."

The first evening one of the Havana friends-of-friends called and said, "Darling, I'm sending a divine man to pick you up. He's a senator—very close to the palace. He's about thirty-five, terribly handsome, speaks perfect English, and is a superb dancer—he'll be there at six to take you to cocktails at La Reguladora."

At six, in the newly acquired white cotton to set off the newly acquired tan, I met my Cuban in the lobby of the hotel. He was dark, muscularly handsome, and gleaming in impeccable white linen. He flashed shell-white teeth at me and bowed over my hand, kissing it as if he were hungry. I simultaneously stepped on his toes, and we were off to a bad start.

We tried conversation over cocktails. He ordered a daiquiri for me and something called "Ol Foshon Con Grondod" for himself.

"Some sort of native drink?" I inquired.

This didn't go well, as it turned out to be an old-fashioned with Old Grandad, and he thought I was making fun of his English.

Then we tried politics, and even way back then it was a mistake. Of the five major parties extant, his was the only one which was right—not just right of center—

but right because it was in. But it was about to be out, and therefore, as he was close to the palace, so was he. The thought of four years' exile in Miami didn't lighten his spirits, and he stared moodily into his Grandad.

After cocktails we drove, through the flower-scented evening, down the Malecon, the wide sweeping boulevard along the ocean, and I watched, with fascination, the native fishermen sitting on the sea wall, flipping the brilliant coral-colored red snapper out of the ocean. We passed a rumbling, primitive cart drawn by a patient creature resembling a water buffalo, and I inquired what it was.

"He is some sort of ox, but resembling in many ways your American mule."

"You mean, like the mule, he'll never be a father?" I said. "What a pity."

He stared unsmilingly straight ahead. Obviously I had gone too far. Apparently Cuban ladies did not discuss genetics with near-strangers.

We drove in silence on through the scented evening and then I said, "What a heavenly smell! What wonderful night-blooming flower has such a scent?"

"It's not a flower. It's my perfume," he answered matter-of-factly.

I may have been taken aback, but I had for the first time opened a subject of mutual interest and he warmed to it.

"You like it. You shall have some," he said. "The store is closed, but I will have it opened."

He wheeled the car around, drove along the Prado, and stopping at a little shop with a light in the back, he jumped out of the car and banged on the door. When the proprietor came, my friend stood, hand on hip, talking to him and gesturing at the perfume-lined shelves. As I watched him, my obtuseness cleared away and I realized why my charm had not proved irresistible to him. It wasn't that I was not lovely. It was just that he was lovelier.

The perfume proved a bond between us which resulted anyway in a splendid friendship and several evenings at the ballet. The perfume also resulted in another bond which held the possibility of more than friendship: The following evening, heavily scented, and feeling even lovelier than my companion of the night before, I arrived with my friends at the Casino Nacional and stood for a moment staring at the spectacularly ugly fountain where a ring of heavy-set, middle-aged, marble ladies danced in purposeless abandon. Behind me a pleasant voice with a British accent said, "What do you suppose they have to be so happy about?"

I turned to face an extremely attractive, tweedy sort of man. He was smoking a pipe in a rather consciously casual fashion. My friend introduced us. His name was Tony (we got on to first names immediately). He was a correspondent for a British newspaper, doing a series of articles on the political parties of Cuba.

Tony was asked to join us, said he'd be delighted

to, "for a bit," because he had an appointment with the president later on at the palace. The "bit" lasted through what must have been a week's salary which went at *chemin de fer* at the Casino and the consumption of large quantities of rum there and at the open-air Tropicana night club afterward. Tony was a wonderfully funny, charming, lighthearted character. We danced under the stars, laughed with our friends, and I was having such a good time that when he said, "May I take you back to your hotel?" it seemed too soon. It was. But it wasn't the hour. It was the perfume. And the rum.

Driving back along the Malecon, it suddenly appeared to him a good idea to stop and look at the moon on the water. I was abruptly enveloped in tweed and being kissed wildly.

"Wait!" I gasped. "Please!"

"What for?" He breathed heavily.

"Well," I said, all my New England propriety to the fore, "after all, we've just met!"

"Nonsense!" he snorted. "I've known you all my life, but not as well as I'm going to—is that heavenly scent you or some lovely flower?"

"Me," I answered. "It's a new perfume—a senator gave it to me."

"Umnh," he whispered, sniffing. "Are you close to the palace?"

"I was last night," I said.

"Palace!" he exclaimed. "My God, I forgot the date

with the president! It doesn't matter—I'd rather kiss you."

"Than the president?" I said, trying to hold him at arm's length.

"Than anyone!" He lurched at me.

I ducked and then cried, "Tony! Your pants are on fire!"

"You're right!" he croaked. "All of me is on fire, and it's your fault, you set the flame!"

By this time another scent was mingling with my perfume: burnt wool. Tony looked down at himself. Small puffs of smoke were rising from his trousers. "My God!" he screamed. "I *am* on fire!" He leaped straight into the air and over the side of the car.

I watched him hop up and down, beat at himself, reach in his pocket, draw out his pipe, and knock the glowing ashes out of it. I'm afraid it was an overwhelmingly funny sight.

"You're supposed to empty a pipe before you put it in your pocket." I giggled.

He was not amused. "You might at least try to help instead of just sitting there."

"I can't," I said helplessly. "I can't stop laughing."

He beat and cursed and hopped, and by the time he had put himself out, some of the magic was gone.

We drove back to the hotel in smoldering silence. "Good night," he said, "and for this I stood up the president!"

It was too bad. He was really terribly attractive.

He wasn't, however, my last chance in the Caribbean. My friends and I went on to Nassau and were as charmed by the Victorian fussiness of some of its architecture in the lush tropical setting as we were by the combination of primitive crudeness and sleek modern living in Cuba.

The beaches were, to me, the greatest attraction. I found the stretches of snowy whiteness ruffled by aquamarine waves irresistible.

When I was told there was a launch which took passengers to an island that was all beach and palms, where one could spend an entire day sunning and swimming, naturally I was the first on board.

As the launch approached the island of incredible beauty, the motor began to sputter, and by the time we reached the dock, it was almost dead. The captain told us that he regretted it would be necessary to flag down a passing ship to get us off the island, and that if any of the passengers had appointments in late afternoon, they had better return to Nassau on the first ship, because it would be at least six hours before he could return with a repair crew.

We disembarked with a sense of Swiss Family Robinson. I went into the bamboo- and palm-built bathhouse to change into a bathing suit and, when I came out, was surprised to see most of my launch companions running up and down the beach waving scarfs and hats at a passing yacht. The yacht turned, came toward shore, and dropped anchor. To my astonishment, all of those on shore started wading out toward the yacht.

The captain approached me. "You staying?"

"Heavens, yes," I said. "I wouldn't miss the day here —you'll be back."

"Right," he said. "We'll pick you both up at about six—there are only two of you staying. No one else wanted to take the chance of not getting back."

Two of us? I looked around for my companion. I thought of all the college contests of "Who would you most choose to be stranded on a desert island with?" —the grammar had always bothered me so I had never chosen—but this day I searched my soul. There was, at the time, a famous leading man who, for want of a better name, I shall call Fringe Benefit, because that wasn't it. I knew he was in Nassau, and I hadn't seen everyone on the launch, so he might just have been on it. I confess his name crossed my mind.

There was a feeling of electricity in the air.

As usual, I had a loose connection. It wasn't the leading man. It was his mother.

She was a perfectly darling old lady who was combining vacationing with her hobby. Like Miss Gunter, she painted wild flowers. She had brought with her, not only her paints, but a portfolio of her completed works and a scrapbook full of her son's pictures.

Six hours later I knew the Latin name of every flower in the United States, and those of all the other areas she had covered, and was familiar with all phases of Fringe's pictorial life from prone-on-a-bear-rug-with-

43

rattle-at-six-months to prone-on-a-beach-with-co-star-at-thirty-six.

As I say, it's never the time or the place, it's the cast.

A few years ago with my True Love (obviously there had to be *one* time when the wires weren't crossed) I toured Europe.

I had never been to Paris, and incurable romantic that I am (I can't think why), I visualized it differently —Paris is for lovers, that sort of thing. It wasn't that there was anything wrong, just not what I expected. We had a very happy time, mainly because we were joined by six feet three of son. Michael, grown up now, was in the Army and stationed in France. We hadn't seen him in two years. The three of us did everything together, the Louvre, the Eiffel Tower, the Lido, Versailles; the boys even did their laundry together, in the bathroom. Paris will always mean to me sitting on my little balcony which looked out, not on the Place de la Concorde, but on the wall of the building next door. The chestnuts were not in blossom, but the scent of detergent filled the air, and the incessant sound of the gentle drip, drip, drip of the boys' drip-dry shirts will ring forever in my ears: The heartbeat of Paris. "Dacron in blossom—tum-ta-te-ta-da . . ."

We went on to Rome, where the three of us became the four of us, because tall son picked up tiny French strip-teaser. We asked him how he met her, and he said, "She was standing on a street corner. I asked her the way to the Excelsior—it was as simple as that."

Well, it seems that when she was not pursuing her

chosen profession she was very shy. Her parents, she had told him, thought she was a secretary. It then became necessary to spend a great deal of time with her because she felt that we might consider her means of livelihood unorthodox and therefore wouldn't like her.

At the end of four days I was so exhausted from smiling at her to show that I thought the whole thing was *fine* that I looked as if rigor mortis had already set in.

Our last night in Rome, before all taking off on our separate ways—my husband back home, my son back to camp, and me across Italy, to discover it all by myself—we spent at the Florida Club, where the object of son's affections was performing. After paying a large bill, we left him, at three in the morning, to his own devices.

At eight he came into our hotel room, hollow-eyed. "The furthering," he said, "of your son's education. She told me to meet her in the espresso parlor down the street. I waited. Until ten minutes ago. May I assume I've been stood up?"

If she had only stood him up on the *first* night, we could have saved a fortune.

The boys saw me off on the train to Florence, bidding me tender farewells with trepidation born of the conviction that I wasn't bright enough to get there.

"Goodbye, sweetheart," said my husband. "For God's sake, don't buy anything else."

"So long, *Mère,*" said my son. "Now always remember, if you get lost, go to the nearest policeman—they are your friends."

I sat back in my compartment in the train, thrilled by the great adventure, enjoying a spot of aloneness, and staring, enthralled, out the window as the fairy-tale castles and green fields flew by. I was on the Orient Express; some passengers were going on to Istanbul, and as far as I was concerned, I was Marlene Dietrich. I dropped off to sleep with this pleasant conviction and woke, with a start, to the conductor's cry, "Florence!"

I leaped up and clawed frantically for my bags, which weighed a ton, being full of considerable Italian marble and bronze.

A voice to my right said, "Please—I assist."

A man in just the right trench coat, and just the right steel gray at the temples, bowed to me and reached for my bags.

"Oh, thank you," I gasped gratefully. "There doesn't seem to be a porter."

He smiled, showing just the right flashing white teeth. Then he opened the window and threw all my bags out, where they hit the platform with a crash of splintering art objects.

I was too stunned to move, until the train started to, and I raced for the door.

"Thanks loads," I said nastily.

"Prego," he said, retiring behind his newspaper.

Florence was all I had dreamed. I spent the first evening wandering around, looking in windows, and mentally orienting myself for the following day's tours. In the morning I was on the first tour, guidebook in hand, prepared to miss nothing. I sat down in the bus next to a lady who might have been drawn by the late Helen Hokinson. Her neatly wrapped hair was topped by a trim little feather hat, and her round, well-corseted body was all sort of pushed up inside the knit dress, so most of it was on top, like a pouter pigeon. Her expression clearly showed that if the antiquities of Florence were not beneath her, those viewing them simultaneously certainly were.

"Good morning," she said. "I'm Mrs. Howard Harvey Clunch, of Omaha." I introduced myself and she said, "I noticed you in the dining room this morning. I said to myself, 'There is a perfect lady'—one of the few, I'm afraid, around."

I said that I had noticed her also. I wondered if that perfect lady bit was why things always turned out the way they did. Because I saw the writing on the wall. Mrs. Howard Harvey Clunch was mine. All mine.

Through the tours, through lunch, cocktails, dinner: interesting-looking people moved about, met each other, joined each other, and I was with my duenna. We were inseparable, and undisturbed; Mrs. Clunch was a very imposing woman. A widow, she had been taking European tours for some years since her bereavement, searching for something or someone who, body and soul, was the equal of Howard Harvey Clunch. No such paragon, naturally, existed. In me, it seemed, she had found a little of his soul. I was so touched that escape was impossible, and our beautiful relationship continued.

My last morning I ordered a cab and was sneaking out of the hotel, a rat, hoping the sinking ship was still asleep. I almost made it out the door, when there was a wounded cry. Mrs. Clunch, umbrella in hand, bore down on me. I thought she was going to hit me with it.

"You were leaving!" she said. I started to apologize, but she said excitedly, "I wanted to tell you—I'm going on to Venice, too, instead of back to Rome. What train are you taking?" She needn't have asked. It had to be the same one.

"Come on, Mrs. Clunch," I said, "I have a cab waiting. There is fifteen minutes to spare before the train takes off. I haven't yet seen the original 'David' —we'll keep the cab outside the museum, but we must rush."

Hand in hand, Mrs. Clunch and I approached the giant translucent figure of David. The closer we came, the more completely awe-inspired I was. Not so Mrs. Clunch. As we stood, straight in front of him, looking up, the sun shining down through the skylight, bathing the whiteness of the marble in rosy beauty, Mrs. Clunch said, "I told you there was no such man as Howard Harvey Clunch—I take it back. *This* was such a man."

We arrived in Venice, and despite everything I had heard, and pictures I had seen, I was not prepared for the impact of stepping right off the train into the middle of the city. There was a full moon, bright enough to bring out all the colors, and there we were. I was speechless. Not so Mrs. Clunch. As we stepped into a waiting gondola, "It is a night," she said, "just made for us!"

When we arrived at the hotel, I said I'd see Mrs. Clunch later, that I had to send a cable to my husband. It read: "I am in Venice. The moon is on the water, the church bells are ringing, the gondoliers are singing. I'm with Mrs. Howard Harvey Clunch of Omaha. Where the hell are you?"

Actually, in our discussion of those gifted or blessed women who draw romantic dalliance to them, it is important to remember that in many cases they don't even have to leave home: attractive males fly, even to their nests, after them. Salesmen, solicitors, tradesmen come and go, and the pattern remains clear. The electricity is there. My pattern also remains clear.

We have a Fuller Brush Lady.

DON'T

DO IT YOURSELF—

PLEASE!

or

How

to Be Helpless

THE PAINFULLY LEARNED LESSONS from an old house in Santa Monica to an old house in Beverly Hills make mine the voice of experience. The trouble is, you probably won't listen to the voice but will go on your foolish way, and you'll have only yourself to blame. Don't say I didn't warn you.

Disobey that impulse! It is your only salvation. The minute you see a "Do It Yourself" kit or get the idea you could make something out of something, spend the money on a new permanent or call the Salvation Army to take the thing away.

I have found there are two fundamental rules in the manual for survival: First, if you *can't* do it, don't try. Second, if you *can* do it, *don't.*

This is basic, because if you can't do something, you're going to get in a frightful mess trying, and if you *can* do something, someone will ask you to. Just be helpless—it takes practice, but it's rewarding.

Hopefully, a few rules, based on experience, may be useful:

Rule No. 1: Look Out for Oldies.

If "you can't hardly get that kind of thing any more," don't press your luck. Count your blessings. Is there anything more charming than an old-fashioned potbellied stove? Yes, there is—are. I know. I am considered a fairly strong person, unflinching in the face of life's adversities, chin up, bite the bullet, that sort of thing. Now I'm licked, admittedly. Down. Out.

"You mean you're going to let a little old potbellied stove *defeat* you?" You bet.

It happened to me—

It *could* happen to you. And it would go something like this:

You are driving along, minding your own business, when suddenly, out of the corner of your eye, which should have been on the road, you spot a perfectly adorable little stove in the window of a junk shop. Without signaling, you pull over to the curb, driving the man in the car behind you crazy. "Wouldn't this create a wonderful atmosphere in the den?" you ask yourself, and as yourself doesn't answer, three hours later there you are. You and this darling stove (which was only $15.00—what a steal!). Twelve feet of stovepipe, a bottle of blacking, three paint brushes, two pounds of steel wool, a saw, four sheets of asbestos, a keg of nails, and, with any luck, a bottle of aspirin.

Installing your darling little stove would be a perfectly simple matter, the nice man in the shop told you. You could do it yourself. That's where you should have heeded the warning signal. The first thing, he said, was to make a round hole in the wall at the spot where you want the pipe. Fine. But he didn't say how you make a round hole with a square saw, particularly in a stucco wall. So you're inventive. By the time you have had the wall, which you shattered with a sledge hammer, patched, you have added fifty dollars to your original investment. Now you have the stove in place, and you wrestle with the pipe ($27.50) as with a boa constrictor. Each time you put one piece in place another slips out, and the entire thing crashes to the floor—on you. You stagger to your feet, haul off and kick it in a fit of temper—now it will never fit; it's bent.

You call the plumber to bring out some more pipe. He takes one look at the stove and says, "You got a permit for that thing?" Of course you don't have a permit—whoever heard of such a thing?—for this dear little old stove. "Why don't you throw it out and get a good gas heater?" he says, and you answer that you just threw out a good gas heater and bought the stove.

"Well," he says, "I'll fit the pipe for you, but mum's the word. I'd lose my license if anyone knew I fooled with the thing. Personally, I think you're nuts."

After he has made three trips because it was never the right piece of pipe, the stove and the pipe are in place. "So long," he says. "Good luck—I wouldn't be a bit surprised if the whole shebang burned down."

Thanking him for his good wishes, you take the steel wool in hand, and a couple of days later there is not one bit of rust on the stove or fingernails on your hands. Then all you have to do is nail up the asbestos, slap a quick coat of paint on it, blacken the stove, and you're ready to light it. The exciting moment arrives, and so does the building inspector who has spotted the stovepipe while moseying down the alley behind your house. He gives you a citation and a little advice. "Don't fool with an old thing like this," he says. "Just go get a good gas heater."

Now you wait until he goes away and like a thief in the night steal back to your stove. It seems to smile at you. The mica windows in its front shine like little eyes, and the wood box at its base, like a jack-o'-lantern mouth, seems to say, "Light me!" And you do. You fool, you. "Pow!" The room is filled with smoke. The front of the stove falls off, little eyes and all, but the brave little stove burns on. You reach for the damper, but you have painted it closed. As the stove gets hotter

53

(and so do you), the blacking begins to burn off, and the room smells as if you were roasting rubber gloves. You wanted atmosphere—you've got it.

And then your smoke signal is received. The building inspector returns. (He has been lurking around, knowing you'd try to pull something.) He throws water into the stove and onto your spirits.

"Didn't get the message, did you?" he snarls, pulling down the stovepipe, simultaneously, you are delighted to see, burning his hands, but not so much as to be unable to write you your second citation, with twice the fine as the first. "What are you trying to do," he growls, "burn down all of Beverly Hills?" (Or Scranton, or Omaha, or wherever.)

There is absolutely no use for leftover stovepipe, but if you look at the brighter side of the problem, by the time you have covered the hole in the wall with a large picture, painted the stove white, and planted it with philodendron, where else could you find a conversation piece so unusual for only $234.75 and a week of your time?

Rule No. 2: What to Not Make into a Lamp. This is such an old story it hardly seems necessary to warn you, but you just may not have been burned.

"Oh, Harry, look at the darling old cranberry picker! There in the antique-shop window—wouldn't it make a wonderful lamp?"

Stop at once. It would not. It would make a terrible lamp. A cranberry picker is for picking cranberries.

A lamp is to light and to look as attractive as possible while remaining lit. The basic shape of a cranberry picker is not particularly interesting unless you are picking cranberries; then you will love it. In the living room it looks rather like a coarse old comb, suitable for use, say, on a horse's tail. Under a ruffled shade it is just plain ludicrous.

The same goes for candle molds, teapots, spinning wheels, samovars, and coffee grinders. I know someone who has looked everywhere for a coffee grinder, because he has a friend who sends him sacks of coffee beans from Brazil. He couldn't find any—they had all been turned into lamps. He finally bought a converted one, at tremendous expense, from an antique shop, removed the wiring, shade, bulb, etc., and had it deconverted back to a coffee grinder. Works fine.

Coffee grinders are functional; teapots are beautiful (one seldom sees a really ugly teapot) as well as functional. It's awful on a chilly afternoon to feel the need of a steamy, aromatic cup of tea and find the pot no longer a pot but a lamp. You cannot pour tea out of a lamp, and there is nothing cozy in saying to an old friend, "May I offer you another bulb?" The only thing that is worse than a teapot lamp is a planted teapot lamp. Which brings us to planting in general.

Plants belong in flower pots, not teapots, doll carriages, old stoves (unless you are forced into it to cover your original investment, as in Rule 1), dresser drawers (even zinc-lined), or the worst possible offenders, which should not, and will not again, be mentioned: chamber pots and cuspidors.

In the same vein, while on the subject of live plants, beware of dead ones: Look out for floating driftwood! In most cases if you see in the water or on the beach a piece of driftwood with a fascinating shape, walk by fast. There are many lovely silvery pieces of driftwood to be had for the picking up. The trouble is, too many people have picked them up and made them into lamps.

If you have found a great piece which reminds you of that wonderful vacation trip, keep it for sentimental reasons, lay it on a shelf or the hearth (if you think someone won't throw it in the fire), but leave it alone and love it.

Rule No. 3: Beware of the Gooey. There are times when I think I may never recover from this period in my homemaking.

All the false friends who tell you how easy it is to do things invariably tout the three worst: wallpapering, floor laying, and working with mosaic tile. These endeavors share similar, and equally unattractive, qualities —they all go up or across something and never quite meet, and they all are applied with an awful goo.

Wallpaper paste is probably the least offensive but the most infuriating. If you take all the advice freely given by the false friends, you will measure and cut the paper first, turn it over, pattern side down, apply the paste to the back, flip it over quickly, and presto! It is stuck—to itself. Now try and unstick it—glad you bought that extra roll? Give up, rumple it up, and throw it away—got it rumpled up, but can't throw it away? Put it on the floor and step on it—now it's stuck to your shoes? Take them off; don't make a problem out of it. Won't come off the shoes? Throw them away too—they needed resoling anyway. There—you have one whole piece ready to hang—hold it above your head, now walk toward the wall, let the top stick first, now sort of lean against it—leaning? Splendid, now let go. You can't? *You're* stuck? Never mind, just stay there—I'll bring this piece over and we'll match the design—oops, my piece is on and the roses don't anywhere near match—I told you to get stripes. What? You're mumbling; I can't understand you—oh, it will wash out of your hair.

Floor laying, whether large sheets or small tiles, amounts to the same thing—the adhesive is not going to be all over it; it's going to be all over you, and it is black, and it *never* comes off. Usually you are installing it in a room with white walls—this enables you to pay a painter twice as much money as you have saved by laying the floor yourself to scrape and repaint the walls.

Now supposing, by some fluke, you have measured correctly, and you have crawled inch by sticky inch toward the corner, and it *fits!* Dont be lulled into a false sense of security, because when you turn the corner, you have to go down a step—this is almost the worst thing that can happen to you. Here's the reason (this is quite technical): all the material used in flooring has something called "Plastic Memory." Now you get to the step—are you with me? You want to bend the tile so it will go over the step. But the tile won't bend, not without the use of a blowtorch—you good with a blowtorch? I'm not. Our curtains went up *Whoosh,* just like that. Lucky the house didn't. Anyway, if you heat the tiles properly, they will bend—and go right over the edge of the step—marvelous! But don't look now—that one is trying to get up. That is Plastic Memory. It seems the little things actually remember they are supposed to be straight, and they're going straight—in some cases commendable, but not this.

The handling of mosaic tiles is, naturally, more artistically rewarding. You can make coffee-table tops (most people make coffee-table tops); you can make pictures (many people make pictures but seldom hang them—attics are full of them), but you can also be tremendously inventive. For instance, we remodeled an old Spanish house (everybody in California where we live remodels old Spanish houses), and in the remodeling I removed some iron grilles from the upstairs windows. The moment they lay horizontally on the ground instead of vertically on the house, I received one of those brain waves that mean nothing but trouble.

I turned them on their sides, put a canvas mattress on one end, and had little table tops made for the other end, which I covered with turquoise-blue mosaic tile. They made splendid combination garden couches and tables. The little glass squares used in mosaic work come stuck to a piece of paper. The easy way to apply them is to spread the surface to be covered with a fierce-sounding adhesive called Grout, then turn the paper over with all the tiles on it. When the Grout is dry, you simply wash off the paper, and there it is, neat as a pin in the same squares as they came in from Italy (they all come from Italy).

But that's not the way I did it. I carefully took each little tile off the paper and placed it on the Grout, upside down, it turned out. It looked strange but rather interesting—until the first rain. Apparently Grout doesn't hold if the tiles are upside down. They are now all over the garden, a colorful reminder of my creative days, along with some Easter eggs the children didn't find last year. The grilles are now back up on the house, because there is a new trend toward Frankly Spanish.

A certain number of these experiences sharpen one's wits. In closing let me just say: Try to learn by the experiences of others, like me. And remember, if you can do it, *don't.* At the risk of speaking with authority, or seeming to brag, I would like to say that, to this date, no member of my family knows I can sew.

THIRTEEN

SAFE RULES

ON WHAT

ABSOLUTELY

NEVER, EVER

TO SAY

TO YOUR HUSBAND

UNDER ANY

CIRCUMSTANCES

or

How to Live with One

GETTING ALONG" with one's husband requires far more than understanding, a desire to please, and an innate ability to look fresh, pretty, and unharassed during domesticity's most trying moments.

It requires a basic instinct on the part of the woman to know not only what to say and when to say it but, more important, what *not* to say, when *not* to say it, and above all, what never, ever to say under any circumstances whatever.

The possible ramifications of not abiding by certain rules applicable to all types of husbands are disastrous. For instance, we may take as an example a wife who reads an article in a magazine dedicated in all good faith to helping the wife to help the husband to help around the house. The ultimate disaster lies not in the article but in its interpretation by the reader.

"Harry and Madge make a game of laying their own linoleum," reads the banner line. "This young Milwaukee couple saved $37.50 when they decided to turn their musty old cellar into a lanai-rumpus room. Now they don't have to belong to a country club in order to have a spot to entertain their friends, and later, what a playroom for the children! They have added to the value of their property, and besides, it was *fun!*"

It was nothing of the kind—as we shall later see in our real case of the wife who didn't abide by the rules.

"One day when Harry returned from the office," the piece continues, "Madge said, 'Darling, we have such a small living room, and there's all that waste space in the cellar—don't you think if we did it ourselves we could make a wonderful room for entertaining?'"

Harry, the piece says, is so proud of the little woman (who isn't little at all; if the pictures do her justice, she's bigger than Harry) that he runs right out and buys yards of linoleum, and they lay the whole floor, using only one hand apiece, because they hold each other's second one during the entire process. This is a neat trick but adds to the endearing quality of the couple. The living room would have been big enough for their guests in the first place if Madge had removed some of those house plants in cuspidors and bird cages she had strewn around. Which is neither here nor there—I'm not quarreling with Madge's sense of décor, except look out! That philodendron almost got you!

Now instead of saying to her husband, "Harry dear, do you think we could do it ourselves?" our real Madge said, "If you'd only stay home once in a while . . ." From then on things go any way but in the manner described in the article. Our real Harry's immediate reaction to being conned into additional work at the end of his terrible day will be one of hurt indignation. "Oh, *sure!*" he'll say. "I have so much time!"

But Madge, being a nag, can't leave well enough alone. "Think of the money we'll save," she adds. This is a sound approach, but Madge doesn't have enough sense to quit when she's ahead. "And you could resign from the club," she goes on. "Just get a guest card to play golf, and we could do all our entertaining right here!"

This tears it. Harry loves the club. It's the only place

he can get away from Madge. There is an unpleasant scene, and the discussion encompasses some recent expenses of Madge's which, if not indulged in, would give them enough money to belong to *two* country clubs.

Nothing more is said about rumpus rooms, linoleum, or country clubs until a week later when Harry has lost a great deal of money playing gin rummy on the commuter's train and is so loaded with guilt that he can't think of anything to say to Madge except, "Honey —about that rumpus room . . ."

Madge moves fast, and when Harry returns from the office the next day there are rolls of linoleum, pots of adhesive, and indiscriminate tools lying about on the lawn.

The weekend finds them as pictured in the article, hand in hand in the cellar. Madge is holding Harry's hand to keep him from cutting the linoleum against the design, which depicts large hibiscus and quite a lot of natives on surfboards. Harry, who now thinks he thought of it, is very excited and can't wait to get started. He has the book of instructions from the linoleum dealer, and he is *ready*. An hour later he has turned over three cans of adhesive, which adhere, swung around while carrying a roll of linoleum on his shoulder, nearly knocking his wife into insensibility, and successfully laid one strip of flooring over some old garden tools which he has neglected to move. The gentle sloping mounds remind him of the fourth hole on the golf course, and he thinks of an immediate errand on the other side of town, leaving Madge to cope with the situation.

At seven he returns home, pleasanter for a day in the open air and three dry martinis. He glides down the cellar stairs, to find that Madge, brick that she is, has almost completed the job herself—she has only one more beach boy to fit into a corner. Instead of saying, "Darling, how wonderful—all by yourself!" he says, "Why didn't you lay it north and south?—the pattern doesn't show—and that end piece is crooked."

In backing away when his wife lunges at him, he trips on a trimming knife, falls, and fractures his coccyx. As the ambulance takes him to the hospital he shouts, "You and your damned rumpus room!"

With the hospital and doctor bills, and the Miltown prescribed for Madge, the floor adds up to approximately seven hundred dollars, and Madge decides she likes French Provincial better than tropical, anyway.

There is a moral to the story: Madge should never have opened her mouth in the first place, without considering first what approach to take. She wants the floor—O.K. The first step should be to make sure Harry does *not* help her with it. How does she manage this? By the simple device of explaining to him how *terribly* busy he is, and that a day in the sun instead of the cellar will be so good for him that it more than compensates for the tiny difference in price between "do it yourself" and professional work—not that Harry couldn't do it better, but after all, he's in advertising, not flooring, and with the pressures of his kind of job, he *must* have relaxation—look what happened to President Eisenhower.

By this time he will be eating out of her hand, feeling *very* tired, and will offer to check into who is the best man to do the job for her. Perfectly simple, nothing to it.

As all of us wives are vulnerable and, though willing, nay, anxious, to please, frequently put our foot or feet in it, as in poor Madge's case, we need help. Therefore I submit, as a public service, a list of rules of what never ever to say which may be safely applied to any type of husband, be he adorable, impossible, lacking in understanding, or full of the milk of human kindness. They follow:

Rule Number 1: This is pretty well covered by the example of Madge and Harry: Never ask him to help around the house. He's likely to.

Rule Number 2: Never say, "Why is it we don't do anything together? We never share things."

When you consider the possible outcome of a statement of this kind, it is blood-chilling. One of two things may happen. He may decide you are right and come to the conclusion that if you have so little in common, why did he marry you in the first place? This is the lesser of two evils because, instead, he may decide to prove you are wrong by sharing his interests with you. Now he takes you to a baseball game and is prepared for the fact that you don't know anything about it, and he is going to be patient, kind, and instructive. He is not, however, prepared for you to ask where the goal posts are. If he is a big man, weathers this, and goes on with the folly, he may say one Sunday, "I have a rather interesting foursome this morning—I might even make quite a piece of cash—how would you like to walk around with us?")

The boys at the club make you as welcome as pellagra, and you trail after them as they tee off, your high heels sinking into the turf, ruining the first green. By the fourth hole you have removed your shoes, embarrassing your husband beyond belief, and you don't know whether they are walking that fast because it's the game or because he doesn't want to be seen with you. When you get near enough to hear what they are saying, they either stop in the middle of the joke, or if they continue speaking, the language involving "bogies," "birdies," and "Nassaus" is totally incomprehensible to you. But you are game, and you are with your husband—or sort of.

By the eighteenth hole you are exhausted, the backs of your legs are killing you, and the fresh little cotton is hanging like a limp rag. You feel the tenseness of the moment and have become interested in the fact which has seeped through to you via the golf gibberish that your husband is about to either win you a swimming pool or lose you your home. All four balls are on the green; the players pick them up, placing coins for markers; the caddy removes the flag from the hole;

the moment has come, and you cry, "Oh, look! Somebody dropped a penny—that's good luck!" And you
pick up the marker of the gentleman whose ball was
nearest the hole. The cost of a new putter to replace the
one with which your husband hits the tree stump instead of you is about that of two tickets to a good show
—and why didn't you get those tickets in the first place,
if you're so anxious to share something with him?

Rule Number 3: Never say, "If you would just stay
home *one* Sunday and help me with the garden, ours
could look as pretty as the Martins'." This is madness.
The gardening jag hits husbands often enough voluntarily, without your risking pushing them into it. All
men have a fertilizer fetish. Let one loose in a garden,
and every new plant, especially the expensive ones, will
be burned to the ground—if a little is good for them, a
lot must be better, mustn't it? Not only will your husband destroy every living thing on your property, but
his timing will be perfect. It will be an unseasonably
hot night, and you will have invited twenty-four people
to dinner, previously working out a menu of hot roast
beef, Yorkshire pudding, and mashed potatoes. You
know the evening is going to be the fiasco of the year.
The house is stifling. Your husband had promised to
get home early to give you a hand filling the ice buckets.
The guests are due at seven, and at four minutes to
seven he arrives, kisses you cheerily as if he hadn't been
giving you a nervous breakdown, and trots out back.
You hear him say to the hired maid who is beefing

about "not a breath of air in this kitchen," "I'll be right in—have to do a little sprinkling." As this is his first constructive move, and you hope will cool off the house a little, you fill the ice buckets yourself and greet your first guest with a wet, clammy hand. Suddenly the guest says, "My God, what's that terrible smell?" And you know. Your helpmate is not sprinkling water; he's sprinkling fertilizer! It is too late. By the time the last guest arrives, you have alternately opened and shut the windows to let in the air and keep out the smell, several times, and nothing works. Dinner is, if nothing else, piping hot, right through to the dessert, which you made a great effort to have served flaming. The guests finish their Cherries Jubilee with a dash of Bandini and a pinch of Vigoro, save their napkins to mop their brows, and after a few attempts at polite conversation, confess the heat has got them, they have early calls, and leave. As the last good night is said, you turn to your husband, screaming, "How could you?" And the poor lamb is genuinely hurt. "But I thought you wanted me to help with the garden," he'll say. Well, you can't say you didn't ask for it.

Rule Number 4: Never say, "How do I look?"

In this case you are wasting both your time and his. If you don't look all right, he will notice it. If you do, he won't. The first sign of a straggling hair, showing petticoat, or crooked lipstick will catch his eye immediately. A new hairdo, loss of four pounds, or a particularly becoming dress—nothing. The best you can hope for as an answer to the question is, "Fine, dear," while he reads the sports page.

Rule Number 5: Never agree with him about his relatives. When he says, "Sometimes I think my mother is crazy," do not say, "She certainly is." He will immediately reply, "Well I don't think you should say that—I don't mean really crazy—" and you will say, "But I do."

Now you are really into it, and presently it will all come out that you have attacked his sainted parent and how could you when she gave you that nice string of coral beads that belonged to her grandmother.

When he says his mother is crazy, just say, "Oh, darling, poor lady, she's old, and she lives alone. We should really see more of her."

"Over my dead body," he will reply, and devote the rest of the evening to proving to you that his mother is off her rocker.

Rule Number 6: This should have been Number One. It is high in importance. *Never* tell him you're tired. *He's* tired. *You* just don't plan your day right. When he comes in after that awful day at the office, kisses you, and says, "How was your day?" *don't* under any circumstances tell him. If you are lucky enough to get a "How are you?" it is permissible to say, "Fine— maybe a little beat . . ." but if you see a glimmer of what appears to be sympathy, do not press your luck, because if you go on with, "I did nine tubs of laundry and was just sprinkling the things down when the kids came home for lunch, and I hadn't even done the beds, yet, by the time I fed them, and did the dishes, I was just starting the vacuuming when the Fuller Brush man—" By this time, if you are not so "on" that you have lost your perception, you will note that a glazed, milky look has clouded his eyes, and he is either making himself a double scotch and soda, opening the lids of the pots on the stove to see what's for dinner, or reading the evening paper. If you pause for breath in your recitation on overwork, he will feel called upon to say something, and without looking up from the paper will mumble, "Well, that's nice, dear."

Just tell your mother you're tired, she knows that if you had married Henry instead, which is what *she* wanted, you wouldn't have to slave your life away like this.

Rule Number 7: Never say, "Honestly, I don't know how Helen can stand it! You have no idea what she has to put up with! Charles is getting impossible!"

You have now attacked a male. You probably don't know about there being a loyalty clause among husbands, unsurpassed by the physician's code of never running down another doctor. If you have friends who are having marital difficulties, the woman is wrong. Your opening statement about poor Helen will immediately be countered with, "Poor Helen, indeed! If she would forget she once had a coming-out party and settle down to being a good wife, stay away from that idiot woman's club, and see that dinner was on the table, there wouldn't be any trouble in the house."

The dangerous aspect of this kind of discussion is that it may suddenly remind him of something *you* haven't done in Wifesmanship. It is all right to say, "It does seem a shame about the Stewarts—I'm afraid they aren't getting on . . ." Then you are on safe ground. You haven't taken sides. There is no point in trying to understand. Just accept it.

Rule Number 8: Never tell him either about a past love affair or about a gentleman getting fresh with you at the dance the other night. In the first case, if he is really fond of you, it will make him mad that the other fellow saw you first. If he is a little bored with you, and the subject, his only answer will be, "Well, if he was so all-fired great, why didn't you marry him?" This can end in tears.

In the second case, he just won't believe you. He will not be jealous, which is what you had hoped for; he will think you are making it up just to make him jealous, which you probably are. Nobody gets fresh with anybody unless there is some kind of encouragement from the other party. Shame on you!

Rule Number 9: Don't ever start any sentence with "Never mind, I'll do it—" or "Aren't you ever going to—?"

First, you'll have to. Second, he isn't. These are the two most bullhead-making approaches in marriage.

Rule Number 10: Don't discuss the price, number, or quality of his apparel. His clothes are a basic necessity. Yours are sheer frivolity. Everybody at the office has more suits than he has—Ed buys four a year. If you rotate them, they last twice as long. But did you *have* to have that dress, and if you did buy one why not black? There is nothing as really smart as a good black.

There is a rider to this rule. Once he has the clothes, look out for discussions about the laundering of shirts. He knows more about the subject than you do. After all, before he was married, and had that nice cleaning woman who washed and ironed his shirts, he wore them for years at a time. He *knows* what's good for the shirts—*knows,* do you hear?

Rule Number 11: Never ask him if he enjoyed his nap after he has snored his way through an entire evening of television. Just help him quietly to his bed. He was *not* asleep: he was just resting his eyes. He heard *every* word of it.

Rule Number 12: Never tell him your dreams. As a matter of fact, never tell anybody your dreams. Somebody may have a knowledge of psychiatry, and it may be your husband. I woke my husband one night and said, "I just had the most horrible dream—I was having a serious operation, and I was alone, in a big, strange, dark hospital, in a strange city—I was crying for you, and you didn't come. It was awful, they couldn't find you anywhere."

He just rolled over and said, "Did you try the club?"

Rule Number 13: By way of summation: *Think* before you speak. You don't know what has happened to him just before. If you have bought a hair ribbon at the dime store, and he has just had a run-in with the boss, he is going to think you are extravagant, and what does he work this hard for, if you are going to throw it all away? On the other hand, he may have put through a big deal, been complimented not only by the boss, but had his secretary tell him he reminds her of Rock Hudson. In which case he may say, "I think it's high time you had a fur coat." You never know. It's all in the timing.

Try to case the situation before you commit yourself to any kind of a statement. The only thing is, don't think too long without saying anything, because then he is going to say, "What are you sulking about? You haven't said a word since I came home."

PRETEND

THEY'RE NOT WITH YOU

or

How to

Drive Your Master Crazy

I AM as fond of animals as the next person, provided the next person happens to be a big-game hunter armed with an elephant gun.

It hasn't always been that way: there was a time when I walked in the footsteps of Saint Francis, the animal lover par excellence, the devotee, the patsy, the pigeon. And speaking of pigeons reminds me of a story which really has nothing to do with this, except that it is a perfect example of how a *worm* (in this case a man) can take just so much before he *turns*. I don't know this man—he is a friend of friends—but my admiration for his inventiveness is boundless.

It seems he lived in an apartment in New York

which was very popular with pigeons, and they knew their rights, which included, by arrangement with a former owner, his window sill. This man, a writer and a kindly fellow, didn't mind the pigeons when he first moved in, thought they were cute—then he made the mistake of tossing them a piece of bread. Well, one thing led to another, and word got around that there were handouts, and from then on there was no peace—not at any price.

Now, as he sat at his desk, trying to concentrate, the feathered, rainbow-hued army marched and clucked on the window sill. Shutting the window was useless: in frustration, the army of occupation was more insufferable. The soft bodies pressed and pecked at the window—the pecking louder than the typewriter —until the writer stopped writing. The complaining voices of the pigeons, in that urgeldy-urgeldy-oh-my-aching-back noise they make, finally turned the tide . . . he yelled at the pigeons . . . he rolled up pages of his manuscript and hurled them at the pigeons, to no avail—a few birds fluttered up and fluttered back, hungrier from their short flight.

Then all of his native intelligence came to the fore. "This is not the way to do it," he said to himself. "Campaigns are not won by headstrong actions—they must be planned—find the enemies' weak spot, that's what you must do."

The weak spot turned out to be salted peanuts—he tried everything until he finally hit it. They were insane about salted peanuts—absolutely mad about them—took to fighting among themselves over them. "Aha!" said the campaigner, "the first step is won—divide and conquer—never fails." He gave them *lots* of salted peanuts so the word would get around to all the little feathered enemies—then came his great moment!

At the crack of dawn he rose and sneaked to the campaign ground. (The pigeons were late sleepers and didn't arrive until they thought he was up, so they could get his breakfast.) He took out a large bag of salted peanuts and, with infinite patience and care, placed peanut by peanut on the sill and strongly and firmly secured it with scotch tape. Then he went into hiding.

The first echelon flew in and fell to—then fell off the sill. Recovering in flight, they returned, and pulled and yanked, and fought and scratched, and glared beadily at the nuts and each other. More arrived, and the scrambling and flurry continued. Feathers flew—pull-yank-pull-yank—until finally the leader said, "Boys, we're licked—tell the others," and one by one they all flew away—sort of sobbing.

Victory was sweet, until the writer returned to his desk—it was quiet—too quiet. He had to think of another excuse for not finishing his novel.

Which proves my point: Take on an animal, and you can't win.

My unconditional surrender has been brought on by years of living with voluntary and involuntary pets.

The voluntary I collected myself from childhood on; the involuntary, my children collected and I am afraid, in one instance, may continue to. My son Michael, now grown and in the Army, is fairly safe, unless he comes home with a mule. My young daughter has a long way, heaven forfend, to go in the field. But the worst of the involuntary pets are not those you or your children collect; it's the ones who collect *you*.

If you go to the pound (don't, ever—you'll come home with them all) and a puppy gives you the *look* which means "we were made for each other—take me—" You do and then he takes *you*. From then on, you are not *his* master; you are not even your own.

Worse, even, are those that come, hungry (or say they are), to your door—a large sad dog or a small sad cat—it doesn't matter, the act is the same. You let it in, your first mistake—hasn't this happened to you before? Of course it has—but you never learn, do you? But you are going to control yourself; you are *not* going to be soft; you are going to just give it that milk (or that chop you were saving for lunch) and send it on its way. Aren't you? *Ha!* You are not going to do any such thing, because the cat, or dog, has either rubbed against your leg, or licked your hand, and you think it is saying "Thank you." What it is saying is "sucker"—it knows one when it sees one. Then you make your second mistake, and two is all it takes. You, or your child, says, "It looks like a 'Charlie' (or 'Fluffy,' or even 'Rover')" —the animal has a name—and you have an animal.

77

There is no exception to this proven rule—name it, you've got it.

It was like that with Willow—Pussy Willow, that is. It was a cold night, not fit for man nor beast, when she knocked at our front door. She did, literally, knock. When we opened the door, she walked in, stiff-legged and wary-eyed, casing the joint. Apparently we passed muster, because she moved toward the kitchen.

She was a mottled black-and-white cat, most of the black on her head, with the exception of long, stiff, white whiskers which stuck out like antennae on each side of her face. She was a very common cat, except for her front paws on which she walked like a tired ballerina in toe shoes which were too small. Later the veterinary referred to "retracted tendons—she may have been born with them, or it may have been an early accident—doesn't bother her a bit."

My husband watched her cross the floor and started to laugh. "That must be the only cat in the world that can stomp," he said.

"Here, Pussy," said my daughter. "What's your last name, Pussy—Willow?"

As simply as that she was ours—all ours.

Willow was really hungry. Our hearts went out to her as she gobbled everything on the plate, and yowled for more. It was after several days of her clunking in and out of the kitchen on a schedule of demand feeding before the reason for her insatiable appetite became clear: she was eating for six. She retired, with ladylike propriety, under the house and gave birth to her family.

The only trouble was, she located a spot between the foundation and the floor, where she put them in, but we couldn't get them out. We might have left them there until they chose to come out, but our dog was so hysterical about their being there that he tried to claw his way through the floor to them. This necessitated calling a carpenter, who ripped up the floor, while we all breathed down his neck, for fear he might hurt the kittens. With great difficulty, and considerable cursing from the carpenter, not an animal lover, he extracted the kittens, but only after we had pulled Willow off him because she was fighting like a tigress protecting her young. Her stubby little claws flew, the kittens mewed, and the carpenter yelled, "Get that crazy cat out o' here if you want that floor put back!" It was all terribly exciting; our daughter loved it. But it was expensive. By the time we had taken Willow and the kittens into a room with a lovely basket and blanket, and shut them in, the carpenter had started to put the floor back. However, it was an old floor, whose boards were narrower than modern floors, so special boards had to be cut to order. We walked around the hole for a week; the carpenter returned; the floor was refinished, and the rug layed.

In the meantime Willow, like a crotchety convalescent, was either demanding to be let in or out of the room constantly.

With enormous relief, the day her enemy, the carpenter, left, we opened the door and said, "Willow, you are free to come and go." She went.

That night, as we innocently slept, she removed the kittens, one by one, and put them back under the floor where she had them in the first place. She knew what was right for her children and she absolutely *hated* that nice blanket.

The second time we called another carpenter—we didn't have the courage to face the same one. It was just as expensive, and Willow was just as mad. Back with her brood in the nice basket, she caterwauled and clunked in and out, until even the children began to lose sympathy for her.

When the day came that the kittens were old enough to be given away, the whole family had had it. Both children worked on their friends, and we on ours, until there was a fine home for each of the six kittens. Everybody was happy, including Willow, who appeared never to miss them. We had just started to relax, when a series of awful noises rose nightly from under the house. It was clear that Willow was entertaining and that we were going to have to go through the whole thing again.

"We simply can't afford it," said my husband. "Why don't I just take her to the club—she's a great mouser, and they'd love to have her at the stable—she really isn't a *house* cat anyway."

"True," I said, "she's an under-house cat. The children won't miss her much. She's never been terribly friendly anyway—I think she's just been using us."

There was no good in my trying to convince myself. I couldn't look my husband in the eye as he drove off, Willow sitting on the back of the seat, like a dowager in a town car, happily going for a ride. Being a party to taking her for a ride was as rough on my husband as it was on me.

He came home that night from the country club, pale and depressed. I said, "Well . . . ?"

"It was awful," he said. "I gave the grooms some money, told them how good a mouser she was, but to feed her well anyway, and then I told them to pat her while I drove away—but she looked over her shoulder at me—reproachfully. I was so upset I played as if I'd never had a golf club in my hand—and we had a lot of money on the game. On every back swing I could feel those eyes—burning into me. I figure she's cost us another couple of hundred dollars."

Willow was constantly on our minds during the following week—how was she faring? Were the grooms good to her? Then one night we were having a dinner party, and there was a knock at the door—a very special knock. My husband and I looked at each other.

"Come in, Willow," he said.

I opened the door.

She clunked in, viewed the company as if she didn't care for it, and stomped out to the kitchen. Then she went under the house and started entertaining her own company.

"And the club is seven miles away," said my husband, marveling. "Obviously we'll have to sell the house to get rid of her—which is not a bad idea, actually. I've been thinking about it for some time . . ."

So we sold the house and moved away, but only after we had given the people who bought it a far better deal, because they were kind to animals and said they'd keep Willow—providing we paid for an operation on her to prevent further floor ripping. We put it all in the contracts of sale.

When last heard from, they liked her fine, except she wouldn't let their great Dane in the house.

There is also the basic matter of keeping out of jail if you are a pet owner.

At the moment we have a relatively small pet population at our house—one poodle, one Siamese cat, and one chameleon. I say relatively, because there have been times when our household included eight white rats, eleven rabbits, four turtles, three cats, two grown poodles with a litter of eight puppies, a snake (this was the worst—it's really awfully hard to get to love a snake), and an owl that walked up and down stairs. It was the best, this owl—it walked flat-footed with a slap-slap-slap like clown shoes. When it reached the top of the stairs, it would just sit there, happily opening and shutting its lime-drop eyes, like the lens of a camera. After all those pets, a cat and a dog and a little old lizard shouldn't really be too much trouble, should they? No, they *shouldn't*—but *are* they? *Yes,* they *are.*

It's because they are crazy about being arrested (not the chameleon—he stays pretty much confined to quarters; he has other drawbacks—we'll get to him later). The poodle, Doc—so called because he has a "what's up?" expression—not only loves our family passionately, he loves everybody's family passionately. So he devotes his entire day to checking on the neighborhood and the neighborhood's garbage cans (he wants to make sure they eat well). In the process he knocks over the cans, and some malcontent reports him to the police. The nice policeman brings him home.

Wagging his tail with pleasure at the friend he's brought to meet the family, Doc licks the hand which is signing the citation.

So, in order to avoid the constant recurrence of police-escorted returns to his home, followed by stern warnings and fines, we built a fence for him. But it was spring, and something was in the air, something so strong that the fence wasn't high enough. Daily Doc jumped the fence and crossed three streets to visit the house of some infinitely patient people who owned six poodles. As Doc's name and telephone number are on his collar, these nice people would call me, I'd stop my nice work, or get out of my nice warm tub, and go get him.

Aside from the nuisance to both parties, there was now the worry of the street crossing, and we lived in constant fear of his being hit. On the advice of our veterinary, Doc went into surgery to lessen his interest in lady poodles. While he was in the hospital, we added two feet to our fence to keep him in, and the nice neighbors put up one to keep him out.

The day he returned he jumped ours and theirs, and they called me. "Come see this," the nice people said as I arrived in a state of fury at my animal. I followed them into a back room in the center of which was a large box containing a mother poodle and a litter of puppies—and Doc, who was sitting in the middle of the lot, smiling happily. "It seems," said the nice neighbor, "that he hasn't been coming to call on the young ladies but the old one—he loves being here with her and the babies. He must have been taken from his own mother too soon."

I knew that Doc was neurotic—but a poodle with a mother complex was almost too much. We decided to take him on a leash when he went out and lock him in the house when we went out. Now we have three more citations from the City of Beverly Hills where we make our home, for howling. Aside from missing his mother, he apparently misses us so much that he simply screams steadily when we leave him. People report to the police that someone is beating a dog, and if this continues, someone may.

So now we have this nice dog-sitter, and I manage my life around leaving the house only when she is available. It's confining, but there seems to be no other way out.

On the other hand, Mo, our Siamese, doesn't miss us at all when we're out—too busy, has a rich, full life, and is completely emotionally and physically secure.

Mo is short for Monarch, because that's what he knows he is, of all he surveys, and people had better step lively. Food had better be on the table, and whatever is, is wrong—send it back; it's not what I ordered; I said liver, not fish. He stalks around looking beautiful and knowing it and sitting only on the cushions which are the best possible coloring for him.

He and Doc play inventive games, preferably for audiences—both are terrible hams. The favorite game is with a paper bag—Mo gets in, and Doc picks up the bag in his teeth, carrying the cat around in it. This is always a smash with guests, but when Mo tires of it he has a number of more delightful games to keep my life ever a challenge.

Like Doc, he adores us, but Mo is also gregarious— in an offhand way. We live across the street from a little park, which the city believes it owns. It doesn't; Mo does. He pads across to it each morning and sits on the edge of the fish pond studying the fish. As people arrive, he joins them, first stalking by with a "you'll be lucky if I speak to you" attitude. Then, after playing hard to get for a little while, he allows the innocents to join him. He is willing to share a little snack, because he's absolutely *famished*—the people where he lives *never* feed him. He then gets into an adoring one's lap and looks up, the incredible blue eyes bluer from the reflection of the sky. "He likes me!" the adoring one says. "Oh, he must be someone's pet—he's so lovable."

So the adoring one finds the telephone number on the lovable one's collar, tucks him lovingly under the arm, and drives *way* across town and telephones me. "I'll be right there," I say, wiping the soap out of my eyes from the shampoo I had been having. Wet and uncomfortable, I drive across town and pick up my beast. The adoring one says, "If you don't want this wonderful cat enough to take care of him, I'd love to have him." I explain that I love him very much, that it was very kind to rescue him for me, but that our house is twenty feet away from the little park, and left to his own devices, he would have returned home.

Having children of his own (ours, but he thinks they're his), Mo is inordinately fond of them. Which makes his gregariousness more expensive. He joins little boys, who take him home, call me, and then have to be rewarded. But the worst part is the reproach of the parents who look at me and say, "He's so affectionate, the children are crazy about him—if you want to get rid of him—"

"I wouldn't think of getting rid of him," I snap, confirming their worst suspicions of my meanness. "I also am crazy about him, my children are crazy about him, my husband is crazy about him, my housekeeper is crazy about him, our poodle is crazy about him—"

"Poodle?" say the children's parents. "Not the black poodle with the white spot under its tail?"

At this point I know they are closing in on me. "Well, yes," I say, "he does have a funny little white spot—"

"And runs loose all the time? He comes to our back door—I think he's hungry—"

"He is *not* hungry," I scream. "He stuffs his face all day long, he only gets loose because he jumps the fence —but we love him anyway, love him, love him—" And I throw my cat over my shoulder and run, sobbing, out of the house, with a sort of a "tsk tsk tsk" sound ringing in my ears.

I tried keeping Mo with me while I wrote, so I wouldn't have to stop and retrieve him, but that didn't work because he sits on typewriters—it makes plot construction difficult.

So I resigned myself to the fate of being at his constant call—I retrieved him from the Beverly Hills Post Office at seven in the morning in my nightgown. Two sweet little boys took him there and called me, then he got loose in the building, and we had to chase him. It's very difficult to explain why you are running about the halls of a public building in your nightgown. I bought a fortune in merchandise from the local hardware store because Mo had gone shopping there (I can't think what for) and they tried to catch him. He escaped through the glassware—it said it was ovenproof; it was *not* Mo-proof.

But things didn't begin really to *get* me until I heard a terrible screaming outside one day. It was obviously Mo, whose voice, loud even for a Siamese, was unmistakable. I ran toward the street in terror, fearing that even though he was clever, a car might have gotten him.

He wasn't in the street. He was above it, in the top

of a very tall palm tree. He had gotten up there—now, he felt, it was up to me to get him down. His howls of rage attracted a sizable crowd of people, including the gardener from next door who brought a ladder. It wasn't tall enough, so there was nothing to do but call the fire department.

An hour later the firemen were still trying to get him down, but he wouldn't come, no sir, not Mo—he wanted Mummy to go for him. So vertigo and all, I went to the top of the ladder. He purred happily while sitting on my head all the way down the ladder, Doc barking joyfully the while at the fun.

After I gave the nice firemen some coffee, the day was pretty well shot, which necessitated working that night. Very late I fell into bed and into an exhausted sleep, from which I was wakened by howls from under my window. Mo, who used to sleep indoors, had taken to demanding to be let out at four in the morning, an inconvenient hour. So we decided to let him stay out, at which point, at four in the morning, he wanted to come in. And this particular morning something snapped inside—I leaped straight up out of bed, scaring my husband to death, grabbed my water glass from the table, ran to the window, in a fury, and threw the water out—the window was closed.

Well, by the time I had dried myself and my husband off, I had cooled down a little; in fact I was pretty well chilled.

There's no point in keeping score—they're always

going to be ahead—even the chameleon. When I was a child, even as short a time ago as when my son was a child, chameleons always died or escaped. But not today. Not today. Today you have these attractive terrariums (miniature gardens under glass—brandy snifters work well) for them. You can landscape them —Japanese is attractive (particularly if you have a Japanese gardener small enough to do the gardening). Today there is no problem about catching flies for the chameleons. You feed them frozen worms. They are a special kind of frozen worm, flown in from Florida —you keep them in the refrigerator until feeding time, then take out the little container in which they are packed in sawdust, where they have been hibernating, sprinkling the rug liberally with the sawdust. Then you reach in with your finger tips and pull one out because your child can't bear to touch it. Drop it into the warm terrarium, where it comes to life—just in time for the chameleon to put it to death.

Our chameleon is a year old and looks fine. The refrigerator problem has been solved. Our housekeeper didn't care too much for the worms sharing the planned dinner, so we bought a small refrigerator where we keep just the worms flown in from Florida and that delightful, but very strong, cheese we have flown in from Canada.

In Beverly Hills people have everything flown in.

At the moment I'm only interested in what can be flown out.

CRUSTACEANS

ANONYMOUS

or

How to Sober Up

a Lobster

The whole thing started with two relatively simple lines of dialogue. It was their juxtaposition which ensnared me. The first line was my husband saying, "The trouble with you is, you take no pride in your cooking."

I was marvelous. I didn't say, "Well, before we were married, I was considered an extremely good cook— you just won't eat anything except chops, steak, and chicken, and you insist on doing them your way, and since you stand over my shoulder throwing a little of this and a little of that into anything else I cook, so I don't know where I am with it, it's no wonder it doesn't taste like anything when I'm through." I didn't cry either. I've been reading these marvelous books on self-analysis which help you to feel everyone else is wrong, but you must *help* them. It was only the man's basic insecurity which made him speak to me that way.

"Darling," I said, "you're absolutely right. It's just that you are such a great meat cook, that I've lost the courage to try. I just let you do it—but I'll try to be more inventive." I didn't even say anything about if he had as much to do for the house, the dogs, cats, and children as I did, plus trying to get some *work* done, he might understand why it took a little of the Cordon Bleu out of me.

I was quiet, submissive, and *wrong*. Being wrong is the best thing to be. You can never get in any trouble if you are. It's being right that's dangerous.

Then the second line of dialogue came through, this time on the telephone. "Hi, girl, I'm back," said a male voice. It was a dear friend (or one whom I thought of as a dear friend) who had been on a South American tour. The friend was a dedicated gourmet as well as tourist, and I knew I was in for a succession of recipes as well as quotes from the bases of equestrian monuments.

I sat down. Then I lay down, and half a jealous hour later (I hadn't been to any of the places, or eaten any of the food, and wasn't likely to) he began to wind up the conversation, "and I can't wait to tell you the most fabulous food-thing—hold on, you'll never believe it! In Brazil there's a way of cooking chicken that's the end. I mean really—first you take this live chicken, or turkey, or whatever, and you give it some rum—"

"Rum?" I said, startled out of my lecture-lethargy. "To drink? The chicken?"

"Absolutely," said the friend. "You see, the theory is completely sound. For instance, you wouldn't want your head chopped off, would you?"

"Heavens, no," I replied.

"Well, there you are," he said. "Neither does the chicken—you'd get all tense, wouldn't you?"

"You bet," I answered, "tense as all get out."

"So," he said, warming to the subject, "that's the basis of the whole theory. They give the bird some rum. He gets very relaxed—and pretty soon he just passes out. When he's out, off with his head, and into the pot—every muscle still relaxed, instead of all tense. Therefore he is tender. I'm going to try it once before I have guests —you can come . . ."

"You come here first," I said. "I know you have color slides, and we might as well get them over with—bring them and dine with us Thursday. I'll try to think of something unusual for you. I've just had a lecture from the master on the quality of my cooking—he takes a dim view of it."

"He's wrong," he said. "There's nothing like a good peasant meal once in a while."

"That's all," I snapped. "See you Thursday—don't dress—we'll just eat cake."

Seething at my good friend and my good husband, I thumbed through a magazine to take my mind off my hurt pride. The solution to my culinary problem leaped from the pages at me: "Live Maine lobster flown anywhere in the United States . . ." I sent a money order, and Thursday morning at my doorstep in California eight of them arrived, packed in huge buckets of seaweed.

I dragged the buckets into the kitchen, turned them upside down, and let the lobsters out. They were furious—had had a bad flight, and didn't care for the spot where they had arrived. They skittered around on the floor, waving their feelers, bugging their eyes, and snapping their claws, to the delight of my dog of the moment, a dachshund, but not to me. I had a whole day to live with them.

The instructions said to throw them into boiling water and to cook them for twenty-five minutes. Despite their surly behavior I began to feel sorry for them. The lobsters backed up against the sink and glared at me. They were so tense. *Tense!* The whole conversation came back to me: "How would you like to have your head chopped off?"

Well, for heaven's sake, on the other hand, how would I like to be thrown into a pot of boiling water? My way was clear. My dinner guests were not only going to have Maine lobster, they were going to have *relaxed* Maine lobster. "What a lovely way to go," I thought as I locked the lobsters in and the dachshund out of the kitchen—he was in grave danger of losing his tail.

I went out and bought two gallons of white wine,

one for the guests (who now numbered eight—no point in going through all of this just for three of us) and one for the lobsters.

By the time my husband arrived home that evening, I was ready. White organdy apron over good black slacks, lots of perfume—the only great hostess is the one who makes everything seem effortless. I almost yawned in relaxation over the evening. Then I explained the whole plan to him. If getting chickens and turkeys drunk worked, why wouldn't it work on lobsters?

My husband looked from me to the lobsters, whose dispositions had not sweetened during the course of the day. "You're mad," he said, "absolutely mad—all of you. But let's get started."

He was taking over again, and this was *my* dinner. I started to say so just as I picked up my first lobster, and he swung on me (the lobster, not my husband), sort of hissing, so I remembered what the book said about men liking to feel masterful. "You take him, dear," I said sweetly.

I poured a gallon of wine into a large pot, placed the pot on the floor, and added just a little warm water to increase the vapors. My husband dropped in the first lobster. He sank into the liquid and started to swim. Then his eyes shot straight up into the air and suddenly came as close to crossing as is possible for a lobster's eyes—they banged against each other. Then he waved his claws wildly, hissed, and climbed over the side of the pan onto the floor: an obvious teetotaler. We put him

94

back in, along with some of his fellows. This time he partook slightly. The reaction was the same with the others. First, "I wouldn't touch the stuff—let me out of here—" Then, "Well, maybe, just one—"

By the time our guests arrived, the four lobsters on whom we had been experimenting were lolling about in the wine, their claws around each other, eyes weaving, and hissing a lobster equivalent of "Show Me the Way to Go Home." Their sober fellows were staring malevolently at their outrageous behavior and clapping their claws in a "shame-shame-shame" sort of rhythm.

The guests walked into the kitchen, which by now was inches deep in wine and milling with the splashing lobsters, us, and the dachshund, who had become quite hysterical with delight.

Our articulate gourmet friend spoke first, as a slosh of wine hit his impeccable suit: "If I'd known, I would have worn my sou'wester—what in hell do you think you're doing?"

"You started the whole thing!" I cried. "I figured if it worked on chickens it would on lobsters—it's a great discovery—look at them—did you ever see such relaxation?"

He looked at the pot of lobsters—one waved a claw languidly at him and slipped back under the wine.

"I'll get you all a drink in just a second," my husband said, then turned to me, pushing a wine-drenched lock of hair out of my eye. "Honey, throw a pinch of tarragon in with them."

"How do you know they like tarragon?" I said.

"*I* like tarragon," he said firmly.

"Bay would be better," said the gourmet friend.

"Damn it," I snarled, "who's doing this anyway? Go make the drinks! I don't need one, I'm getting enough by osmosis."

They left me with my lobsters who were relatively quiet, only occasionally suddenly thrashing and covering me and the wall with wine. Then gradually all motion slowed down, and with a common sigh they passed out. I lifted the pot to the stove and turned on a slow flame. When the wine reached the temperature of a warm tub, I covered the pot and walked gently away toward the bar. There was a hollow hiccup from under the lid.

My husband and the guests had had several cocktails by the time I joined them, and he and the gourmet were in a spirited discussion of the future of alcoholic cooking. "As I see it," he was saying, "the success of the meal will depend on who gets drunk first, the host or the dinner."

"The stew or the stewed," chortled the friend. "By the way, isn't it time to start the second batch of lobsters?"

They were taking over again, but mellowed by the wine fumes and half of a martini, I said, "Right—do you boys want to cope this time?"

Authoritatively they moved to the kitchen, followed by the remainder of the guests who waded in, carrying chairs. These boys didn't work without an audience.

I placed the second pot on the floor, where it floated slightly before settling, and reached for the other gallon of wine. It was gone. I hadn't realized I had used that much.

"Never mind," said my husband. "We'll use that bottle of California brandy out of that awful Christmas basket your cousin sent us."

"Your sister," I said. "It's corky, too."

"The lobsters won't mind a little cork," he said gaily, "will you, boys?" He poured the full bottle into the pot and added some warm water. Then, aided by the increasingly helpful guests, he placed the remaining lobsters in the brew.

Hell, apparently, hath no fury like a lobster in brandy. They leaped, hissing, over the edge of the pot, and clattering out onto the floor, charged like armed juggernauts in every direction. One got the dachshund by the tail, one the cuff of my husband's pants. By this time the undamaged guests were laughing so hysterically that they were of no help.

The angry lobster quadrille continued until my husband bravely tossed them one by one into the wine after removing their already cooked brethren. They finally subsided, but went down fighting, knocking reproachfully on the lid until the end.

Dinner was delicious. It was easy to tell the difference between the relaxed and unrelaxed lobsters: the first batch was sweet and soft, the second stringy and sort of cross-tasting. Or maybe it was our imagination—

we were all a little unnerved by the experience so we had quite a little wine with dinner.

The whole thing was a smashing success. My husband said I had certainly taken pride in my cooking, which showed not only ingenuity, but just plain guts.

My gourmet friend was so enchanted that when he left he said that, as soon as he got his strength back, he was going to try it on a turkey.

The following week the telephone rang. It was the gourmet.

"How are you?" I said. "Have you gotten to the turkey yet?"

"I am not well," he said hollowly. "The turkey got to me. You see, after the awful experience with the brandy, I decided to stick to rum. This turkey took it like a man. Then I had some, then I gave him some more, so pretty soon we were drinking together—what a capacity that bird has! Well, one thing led to another, and pretty soon the two of us were loaded. Now, you know, you just can't suddenly take an ax to a drinking companion, particularly such a nice one. The upshot of the thing is we both passed out, and we both woke up with hang-overs. Now what shall I do?"

"Come for dinner," I said, "and bring your friend."

I'm rather looking forward to it. Any friend of a friend is a friend of mine. We're having parched corn. I hope my husband likes it—it's hard to get.

THE CASE

OF THE BLACK THUMB

or

How to Let

Your Garden

Cultivate You

IN THIS TROUBLOUS TIME of history when shifting values, changing hem lines, world weariness and space fears fill us with an abounding sense of insecurity, man—or woman, for that matter—in frequent cases turns to the land for comfort and assurance in the future. To get his feet back on the ground and his hands into the earth.

After all, what is more gratifying, more truly soul-satisfying, than returning to the soil, to plant, to care for, and to watch things grow?

Anything is.

Say lunch with a friend, a good matinee, or, for that matter, a bad cold.

Admittedly, I have a black thumb. They say if you love plants you can make anything grow. I love them. They just don't love me. With the exception of weeds, anything I touch withers and dies. Anything, that is, in the category Flora. Fauna, now, is a totally different proposition. As clearly established, cats adopt me, dogs adore me, even white rats lie still and trusting in my hand. And this attraction is not limited to the domestic breeds. As I move on my appointed garden rounds I am followed by a veritable covey of twelve-footed and no-footed little friends, snails and caterpillars predominating. That is, they follow me if they haven't gotten there before me, making lacework of the new acanthus leaves. Then they just smile—with their mouths full.

The snails are the worst. They know you can't bear to step on them. But you *must;* it is a simple matter of survival. You or they. It took months for me to gain the courage to start stepping on them. And now the most terrifying thing has happened. They're back— *without* their shells. Someone said then they're called slugs. But I know better—it's the same group. I can tell.

One of the great joys of a garden is to explore it in the early morning, when the dew is on the grass, and the blossoms haven't yet quite wakened to greet the day. It is a magic moment. Tiptoeing over to an exquisite bloom just beginning to turn its face to the sun, I look deep inside its cup, almost expecting a fairy to look back at me. It isn't a fairy. It's an earwig. An earwig, in case you are lucky enough to be unfamiliar, is a quite small but very repulsive long scaly insect. He looks back at me all right. Challengingly. He knows whose flower it is. Never quarrel with an earwig.

The following quotation from a gardening manual exemplifies the futility of an argument: "The earwig population in California has increased as rapidly as the human population," it says. "These bugs have favorite foods but will accept a wide variety of others. When conditions are right, they even move into the house."

Accept! "Please, Mr. Earwig, try just one little bite of this new Brazilian orchid. You may find the flavor a little piquant at first, but once you get used to it, you won't want anything else. We can have them flown in for you. Anything we can do to alter conditions in the house that will make it more acceptable to you, just speak up. I hate to see you lying there on that cold camellia."

The manual suggests that if you do *not* wish to bend to the will of the earwig, there is only one way out: Total War. The secret weapon is their *product.* I bought the product and prepared for the holocaust. Slipping into a mechanic's uniform, rubber gloves, and a riveter's helmet (anti-fallout measure), I rose at dawn and approached the earwigs' stronghold. It is easy to tell where they are, because after they have been at work, the flowers just give up, turn black, and fall down. Attaching the spray nozzle to the end of the hose with some difficulty, I opened the jar in which the product was to be mixed and read the directions: "May be fatal—avoid breathing while using." I followed the directions to the letter, made the mixture, spraying the entire area, while simultaneously avoiding breathing, and by the time I reached the end of the flower bed, *I* was ready to turn black and fall down. The earwig was fine. So much for earwigs.

Caterpillars are more complicated and consequently more challenging. Stepping on them is unthinkable, because they are so cute and fuzzy, and your child will scream, "Stop! It's my friend!"

I have met the caterpillar's challenge in a way you may find useful. The maneuver is elaborate but infinitely worth while. It involves patience, ingenuity, and two coffee cans with tight lids. The night before you put out all the anti-caterpillar pest-control remedies on the market. The caterpillars love them and will come from everywhere just to get a little. In the morning you call your child (should be a rather young one, say under seven; they get crafty as they get older—can be a boy or girl) and you say, "Heavens, will you look at all our furry little friends. Why don't you see how *many* you can collect?" The child falls to at once, and you slip away to do some errands. You return; the child is triumphant; the can is full of nice, live caterpillars, and you cry, "Aren't you marvelous? Let's get an ice-cream cone—go wash your hands."

The child races to the bathroom; you rapidly place

the can of caterpillars in the trunk of your automobile and replace it with the second can in which, in the meantime, you have placed either a doll or a boat, depending on the sex of the child. (Care must be taken that the weight of the toy approximates that of, say, sixty caterpillars. Just guess at it—I don't have that figure at hand.)

Now off you go with your child—or anybody else's —to the ice-cream parlor where you buy a double cone, unless they have triple ones. You drive slowly away so that the ice-cream begins to melt. By the time it reaches the upholstery, you cry out to the child, "Oh, what a mess! And chocolate is so hard to get off. I think I have a towel in the back of the car."

At this point speed is essential. Stop the car, leap out, open the trunk, grab the can of caterpillars (you *have* been careful to make sure the lid was *tight?*), drop the can quietly into one of the refuse tins lined up for city pickup. Get back into the car quickly, and get the child home—you *did* forget the towel. Once home, mop up, remove the lid from the second can, and say, *"Look! They've all run away, but they've left you a present!"* If the lid wasn't tight and they *do* run away, they are blocks from home. The child is happy with its reward, and as far as the trash collection is concerned, you pay your taxes, don't you? As I say, it's elaborate, but it works.

The same useful manual which deals with garden enemies states that a sensitive gardener is attuned to the rhythm of plants. "The fast action beat of a plant in the sun and the slower rhythm of a plant in the shade can determine the plant's need of fertilizer."

When I went into the garden and listened for the rhythm, I tuned in immediately. It was marvelous. Not exactly rock and roll, but a kind of symphony of the flowers crying out for fertilizer. They seemed to be saying, "Feed me." Listening to them was my first big mistake. I started for a seed store to purchase the product recommended in the manual, but on the way, from the car radio, came a sort of doom-shaped voice saying: "Is your garden dead and dull-looking? The answer is bat guano—the richest, oldest fertilizer in the world—aged two thousand years in caves." Throwing loyalty to the manual to the winds, I hastened to the store and bought the bat guano.

On reaching home, I dug right in. Sometimes it's wonderful to really get your hands into the soil, not to mention elbows, face, and hair. Having covered quite a large area with the prescribed number of teacupfuls of the ancient droppings, I watered everything carefully, retired to the house, bathed, and spent an enjoyable evening visualizing myself in chiffon and picture hat, picking the exquisite blooms for my exquisite table.

The next morning I rushed out, prepared to sway with the rhythms of the plants, but it was clear immediately that something was terribly wrong with the part of the garden I'd bat-guanoed yesterday. There was silence and a sort of limp quality to everything.

The snapdragons didn't snap: they didn't even snarl. Everything looked tired. The rhythm started like a lament. The following day everything was lying flat on the ground and had turned brown except one unidentifiable and overpowering plant. I cleared away the dead flowers and centered my concentration on the living plant. It was enormous, a pale, unnatural green, and I swear it wasn't there two days before. Three days later it had grown two feet, and the rhythm reached the crescendo of a march. Eight days later the plant was four feet tall and had turned toward the house. I went for an ax, ran out, and chopped it off at the roots.

As I did, a shadow crossed the sun. I looked up. It wasn't a bat or a vulture; it was just a blue jay, but he was making that noise they do which sounds like laughing. The marching rhythm changed to a dirge. I went out to the garage and took down the box of bat guano and studied the package carefully. It said things about "not in the heat of the day" and "not in a high wind," but it also said tea*spoon*ful, not tea*cup*ful. It seems you *can* have too much of a good thing.

In my lengthening experience I have found that when you buy seeds or plants, it pays to talk to your dealer about your gardening problems. Particularly in the case of watering, which is, of course, all-important. After he gives you your instructions, you return in a few days with the dead plants in your hand.

"How often did you water them?" he will say, probably scowling.

"Every day," you reply, "regularly."

"Too much," he says.

Or it can go this way, as he looks at you accusingly: "How often did you water them?" And you reply, "Oh, about every other day." "Not enough," he will say.

Along with making clear to you who is responsible for the demise of the plants which were perfectly *fine* when they left his establishment, the dealer will give you a brochure full of good advice so that you won't kill any more of them.

This gardener's guide further instructs you to "set out bedding plants, because it will soon be too warm for the delicate blooms." In my case I dutifully "set out" several flats of small plants, mixing in with the flowers some herbs recommended as the method of turning every ordinary meal into a gourmet's dream. The book says, "The combination of flowers and herbs makes an enchanting old-fashioned garden—and why not add a little catnip? It is decorative, has a lovely scent, and if you have a kitty he will thank you to the end of his days." Why not indeed? I have a kitty. He is dictatorial, aggressive, and demanding, and I thought how therapeutic—catnip is said to be not only delightful but satisfying to cats, like a good pipe. Possibly, I thought, if I grow him some, he'll stop howling for sustenance every time anyone walks by the kitchen door.

The morning after I set out the plants I hastened to the garden to see what tiny little green plant had put out new leaves or shown signs of budding. No tiny little green plant had. The tiny little green plants were all lying on their sides as dead as doornails. My kitty *did* love the catnip but had no opportunity of thanking me to the end of his days, because all of his friends also loved the catnip and had spent an orgiastic night rolling ecstatically over it and all the other plants.

The bedding plants, having been put to bed so forcibly, simply decided not to get up.

Now, along with printed material aimed at helping me to make my garden more beautiful, I also absorbed some aimed at helping me to make *me* more beautiful. With rapt attention I read about "Nature's own beauty product—for a lovelier you!"

Beauty from my garden, which had previously been making me old before my time? The piece explained that lemons, if applied directly to the elbows and kept there, would bleach and remove calluses; cucumbers sliced and placed on the face would whiten the skin and refine the pores; sour cream was more beneficial than commercial cold cream for the complexion; and olive oil, one of the world's oldest lubricants, when rubbed into the hands made them smooth as a baby's. The piece finished on a high note: "After bleaching them, rub some oil deep into your elbows. You'll be amazed at the thirsty way they say 'Thank you.'"

Nature's way wasn't easy. The article suggested leaning in the lemons as the best manner for elbow bleaching, but I had weeding to do, and time was a-wasting, so I strapped a half lemon on each elbow with a piece of gauze. I couldn't get the cucumber slices to stay on my face while leaning over so inventively put them and the sour cream in the blender together and made a fine paste which worked like a charm. Spread all over the face and neck, it made a complete mask.

As it was a warm day, there seemed no point in putting the olive oil only on the hands, so I donned a sunsuit and rubbed it all over me. Then I thought better of it, remembered that sun was drying, so added an old pair of pants and shirt of my husband's, wound a rope around the waist to keep the pants up, tied my hair in a scarf, adding a pair of my son's old tennis shoes and some rubber gloves.

I've never been happier at my work. As I wrested the weeds from the soil, I felt the cucumber drawing my pores together, the oil and cream smoothing my skin, and like a caterpillar about to turn into a butterfly, thought of the night ahead in which I would walk in beauty. I took deep breaths as I pulled straight-kneed —*and* one two three pull, one two three up, breathe, *and* throw the clump of weed over the shoulder onto the cement of the patio where it is easy to sweep up. Make an exercise of your job—build a figure as you build a face—one two three pull—my husband will take me out to dinner, I am going to be irresistible—one two three straighten and throw—

There was a muffled cry, and I turned around to face my husband, who was wiping the remains of the dirt clod from one eye. With the other eye he was looking at me as if he had never seen me before and didn't want to again.

"You never looked lovelier," he said. "Like the Bride of Frankenstein—what are you made up for?"

"Well," I said, "it was this article I read, and I thought while I was weeding the garden—oh, it's just too hard to explain—"

My husband made a choking noise and stared, transfixed, at the nice clear place I had just weeded.

"My artichokes!" he cried. *"What* have you done with my artichokes?"

I couldn't have, but I had. They looked exactly like the picture of a weed in the manual.

"Oh, darling," I cried, "I'm so sorry—what a terrible mistake." I started to throw my arms around him, to comfort him—he *loved* those artichokes.

He leaped away from me, shouting, "Don't touch me —I have to wear this suit tomorrow." Then he looked at me with the tears starting through the sour cream and said, "Come on, Black Thumb, I'll take you to dinner—you *are* changing, aren't you?"

Gardening is like anything else—*it's all in the way you approach it*. Positive thinking can see you through. Take my husband, for instance. Understanding my gardening problem, he has bought me what I most need. A gardener.

FILE UNDER S

FOR SENTIMENT

or

How to Stop Them

Before It's Too Late

Help!" screamed a voice from the attic. "Help!"

I went up the stairs slowly. I wasn't worried. It was my husband's voice, and if he stays home from the golf club on Sunday to "do a few little things around the house," he always gets hurt. Never badly. Just enough to warrant a short trip to the emergency hospital, a few stitches, or that sort of thing. Just enough so that it takes all day Monday to undo the few little things he's done around the house Sunday. We try not to discourage him, because we want him to feel he really *belongs*.

"What happened this time, darling?" I said sympathetically, opening the attic door.

The poor man was on the floor, covered by myriads

of pieces of colored paper of all sizes, some of which were still fluttering down, like a plague of locusts, from a shelf above his head.

"Help me up," he groaned.

As I dug him out, he growled, "What in God's name is all this junk? I was reaching up on the top shelf for the electric sander—I thought I'd do that table—and suddenly this whole box of stuff fell on me, and this thing hit me on the head and almost knocked me out—what *is* it anyway?"

He held out a large ceramic blob glazed a bilious green.

"I think it's a horse," I said. "Mike made it when he was in kindergarten."

My husband looked at me. "Michael is now eighteen years old and in the Army and you still *have* this thing?"

"Well, yes," I answered. "I just can't seem to get the courage ever to throw away the things they make."

"Well, right now, sentiment or no sentiment, we're going to start throwing them away. We're losing valuable space, and besides, it's a dangerous fire hazard. Here's an old postcard. You certainly don't want that."

One side of the card pictured a squirrel. Under the squirrel was written, "Greetings from a little friend." On the reverse side, beneath the name of a summer camp our son had attended at the age of seven, was written: "Dear Mom, I hope you are feeling well because I am not. I caught my hand in the washing machine and got all my teeth bashed in. Love, Mike."

My husband laughed, said, "Better file that," and sat down in the middle of the debris and started sorting.

"Better file this too," he said, holding up a finger painting of Meg's. "It's pretty good. Giraffes are hard to draw."

"It's not a giraffe," I said, pointing. In the corner of the picture was written, "A portrait of my father, by Meg."

"Pass," said my husband. "Now look, there is only one way to do this. We'll make a series of piles of stuff. Keep them as chronological as possible. Then, if there are a few from each pile that you just can't part with, we'll file them away."

One day and five nights of hard work later, the piles had spread through the attic door, out into the upstairs hall, and a few scattered specimens made their way into the living room. Meg, with a delighted cry of recognition, had retrieved a soft powdery clay Easter basket, one of her first nursery school efforts, and was playing with it on the floor where it was working its colorful way deep into the nap of the rug. Michael, home for a visit, was mending a cedar chest he had made in the fifth grade. The sawdust and glue flowed toward the clay dust and combined to make a lovely pattern with the pieces of raffia from some YMCA camp woven work that Doc, the poodle, was happily unweaving with his teeth.

"I think you might have consulted me before throwing this out," our son said reproachfully. "It took me three months to make, and it's the only time I ever got a B in shop. After all, I may have a son myself some day, and I'd like to have *something* to pass on to him."

I shifted guiltily.

"Don't tell me there is nothing in heredity," said my husband. "Now, let's get some boxes. You may all take one or two of these precious items from each pile, put them in the boxes for saving, and we'll burn the rest. You'd better get a large box for your mother. I have a feeling she'll need it."

We all filed upstairs, boxes in hand. Michael was the most organized. Army training is marvelous. "I'll never need these any more," he said, tossing a box of Exacto knives, formerly used in the creation of model airplanes, into the box marked "Give Away."

My husband cried, "Don't give those away—I can use them in the toolbox." In retrieving them, one slipped and cut his finger. After the finger was bathed, dabbed with Mercurochrome, and wrapped in Band-Aid, my husband sat down and watched us as we continued our labors.

"Here's an old composition book of yours from the fourth grade, Mike," I said. "That, I think, we *could* throw away."

Michael looked into the book and said, "Not on your life—this is great literature, my first treatise on the history of New York. Listen: 'The Dutch King. Once there was a Dutch King and he was yelling. And he was as mad as the dickens he was bossing everybody around and saying You damn fools and he said we can't go on like this we can't surrender either. The Indians have attacked. Our men are going by the dozens. Suddenly the King heard something it was a tribe of Indians and the King said yank em away. They certainly were hostile Indians because they were throwing spears and knives and everything you could of thought of. But the King won the war.' "

"That's *good,* Mike!" Meg cried. "What's hostile?"

"What I'm going to be if we don't finish this job," I said. "All right, granted, the Dutch King must not go, but now let's speed this up."

Under Father's supervision we filled the "save" boxes with hammered copper plaques depicting tired Mexicans leaning on cacti, woven leather lanyards for wearing a whistle about the neck, considerable Indian beadwork complete with fringe, a balsa-wood wishing well (which leaked) for planting philodendron, pressed seaweed under glass, a dried toad (previously run over and very flat), finally disposed of by Michael and retrieved by Meg, a champagne cork from our wedding supper, and one small white sugar dove from same, a lock of hair from Michael's first haircut, a baby slipper with the toe chewed out by the first puppy, Cub Scout awards, nursery school gold stars, several handkerchiefs wtih "Mother" painted on them in textile paint, and then all these finger paintings. They were the worst.

I sent Meg downstairs on a false errand, and like

thieves in the night we grabbed a bunch of the pictures and stuffed them into a wastebasket along with several pots of flowers cut out of construction paper. But we weren't quick enough. She returned silently, for once, caught us in the act, and screamed, "My paintings! My flowers! That's not very nice," she stormed, dragging them and everything else out of the basket. "All day long in school nothing but cut and paste, cut and paste, and then you throw them away—that certainly isn't very nice. I'm never going to make anything for anybody ever again. I may not even live here any more! I may go in the Army the way Mike did!"

By this time she had both men on their knees, saying, "Don't cry, baby, we won't throw them away. We'll keep them. We'll even frame them! Daddy wants one to hang in his office. Now, do you think a dish of ice cream would make you feel better?"

She thought it might, and Michael started downstairs after it.

Well, it went on that way, really quite an emotional experience, and then suddenly we were through. The "save" boxes were filled to the brim; the "Throw Away" box remained empty.

My husband surveyed the fruits of our labors. "Marvelous," he said. "We have accomplished a great deal. Everything has been shifted from one box to another and nothing has been disposed of. I know when I'm licked. I'm going to call a carpenter and have a proper cupboard made for this stuff. And now."

So now we have this marvelous cupboard. A place

for everything and everything in its place. Deep drawers for ceramic and copper work, small drawers for high-jumping medals and baby teeth, middle-size drawers for raffia objects and lanyards, and a huge flat drawer for works of art from finger paintings to scale drawings of constellations. Michael has just mailed home a sharpshooter's medal, and some subversive element in Meg's school is teaching her to *sew*. Why they couldn't leave well enough alone, I'll never know. And there is no end in sight, when you consider that between Halloween and Thanksgiving we have added to the collection one four-foot paper jack-o'-lantern (for hanging), one eight-inch clay jack-o'-lantern (for placing on table to decorate and remove finish), five Pilgrims, six turkeys—I can't go on.

And Christmas just around the corner!

We have only two children, a fact I have always regretted, except when I consider the ramifications of the creative efforts of a large family and the heartless co-operation given these efforts by the Board of Education.

Therefore, as more or less of a public service, I should like to offer a few suggestions on how to face what comes home from school and how to learn to live with it.

Number One: If you can't lick it, join it. For instance, in the case, say, of a four-foot-square hammered copper version of Rosa Bonheur's "Horse Fair." It is presented to you proudly and lovingly. There is no way out. It must go in the living room. Not there where the curtain can be pulled across it. Out there where everyone can see it. Who needs a perfect Regency room anyway?

Some comfort may be drawn from the fact that time heals all wounds. In about six months an object may be eased from the living room into, say, the library. It will undoubtedly have been replaced by a two-foot vase made entirely of cigar bands lacquered to a base which is both useful *and* ornamental. It won't hold water, but you *must* have some dried flowers around the house. While the change is taking place you will have been wearing the sea-shell earrings or shinbone tie clip anyway, so the adjustment need not be traumatic.

Number Two: Try to persuade both child and teacher to construct something that not only can be used but used *up*. Matches would be ideal, but of course that is out of the question. Something, say, like hand-decorated disposable tissues, or personalized dog biscuit with "Rover" written in harmless vegetable dye.

Number Three: The Accident. This is rather advanced and probably should not be attempted until the third or fourth child when the ruthlessness brought on by desperation sets in.

If the object is large and either clay or ceramic, procedure is relatively simple. As it is handed to you, you say, "How beautiful! A bear! I love bears!"

The child says, "It's a dog."

You then say, "Of course it is. I was looking at it upside down! A police dog, isn't it?"

"It's a beagle," the child says.

Now things are likely to be touchy, and you shouldn't force the issue. Wait, say, for twenty-four hours before you call, "Darling, don't you think that beautiful paperweight you gave me, which is a little large for my desk, would make a wonderful doorstop?" Don't force it; just see how it goes. If it doesn't, you have a paperweight. If it does, it will be no time at all before he kicks it down the steps and breaks it. *He* did it. You are heartbroken. He isn't. He'd forgotten all about it, and it was a crazy old thing anyway.

A word about lanyards. A lanyard, as defined by Webster's Dictionary, is: "A short piece of rope for fastening something in ships, especially one of the pieces passing through deadeyes and used to extend shrouds, stays, etc., *or* a cord worn around the neck by sailors to which is usually attached a knife, *or* a strong cord with a hook at one end used in firing certain kinds of cannon."

You may wonder what you are going to do with a lanyard. Camp counselors sometimes attach whistles to them.

You will get a lanyard. There is no use fighting it. You will probably get several. It doesn't matter whether you have a boy or girl or boys *and* girls. They make them. All of them. At school, and at camp. They just keep making them. You figure out what to do with it, because you are going to get one. You are going to get a lanyard.

TIME

OF

SORROW

or

How to Match

a Goldfish

My son learned to face life, and death, at an early age. I was convinced, with my first-born, that the truth would make him not only free but strong. It was far wiser, was it not, to prepare him to face reality, than to live in a dream world?

It was not. As I watched Michael playing happily under the tree on his first Christmas, I remembered the shattering shock of my childhood, when I was told by a spoilsport playmate that there was no Santa Claus.

My curly-headed baby was not going to suffer as I

had; he was going to *know,* and to understand, and he would not be hurt. He wasn't hurt; he was just plain mad. After four years of indoctrination, too many presents on all occasions to soften the acceptance of reality, he turned on me—like a tiger.

He ran into the room at Christmas time with a soft woolly animal cradled in his arms. "Look what Santa brought me!" he cried joyfully.

"It's adorable, sweetheart," I said idiotically, "and what fun to pretend it was Santa—it was probably Aunt Stella."

"It was not! It was not! It was not!" Michael screamed at me. "And you stop it! I'm sick of your saying everything is the 'spirit of the thing'—I know all about God, and the Easter bunny, and the fairy that gives you money under your pillow for a tooth, and all that stuff—but I don't care what you say! When Santa takes off his suit—there's a man inside!" He hurled the animal at me with considerable strength for his size. It hit me full in the face, and it wasn't nearly as soft as it looked. I must say, I had it coming to me.

One would think, having goofed at life-facing instruction, I would have learned my lesson, but I wasn't learning lessons, I was giving them.

One morning, a few months after Santa had moved back in with us, Michael came into my bedroom before I was completely awake, clutching something in his hand. He opened his hand and dropped the object on my pillow. "What's the matter with it?" he said.

I forced open my eyes and looked directly into those of a goldfish which was quite dead. I gathered myself together, and my robe about me, and said, "Darling, I'm sorry, but he's dead. You mustn't be unhappy, it happens to every living thing sooner or later—we'll get you another."

Gingerly I picked up the fish by the tail, and my son followed me into the bathroom where I disposed of it in the usual manner. As our problem flushed away and vanished with a little glug, I turned and flashed a smile at my son. "There we are," I said, more brightly than I felt. "Now he's gone, and we won't think about it any more, will we? We'll buy a lovely new one this afternoon after school. We'd better hurry—today's the Spring Festival, and you'll be late for your recital."

The Sunnyheart Nursery School's auditorium was packed with perspiring parents. The audience was predominately female, except for the sprinkling of uncomfortable fathers, looking strangely like molting penguins as they wriggled in their seats and ran their fingers along the inside of their collars while waiting for the performance of their progeny.

"We have tried," Mrs. Ludlow, the principal, said, pitching her voice for the last row, and making it, "to instruct the pre-school group in a few basic fundamental facts about the subjects on which they will speak and letting them tell their story in their own way. At Sunnyheart we do not have the child learn his speech by heart, as we feel that if we do so, we intrude on his personality. Now, if you are all comfortable, we will begin. Our first young man is going to talk to us about Abraham Lincoln."

Little prickles rose on the back of my neck as I watched my son walk out on the stage. He looked so small and brave in the trim blue suit. I was so glad I had insisted on the short pants although he had bellowed that *everybody* wore long ones.

Michael bowed to Mrs. Ludlow, hand on stomach, properly, as he had been taught. Then he looked straight out at the audience. "Too bad about Abraham Lincoln," he said. "He was a very good man. He had whiskers and could read in the dark. He liked everybody—he even liked school. He took care of all the people, and freed the dark-faced ladies, and now he's gone down the drain. Somebody will have to buy another President. Thank you."

After explaining the audience reaction to Michael, we gradually straightened other things out, including getting it through to him that our beloved Negro nurse and housekeeper were not representative of an entirely female race and that the disposition of those gathered to their forefathers was not always so simple. It took a little time, and why couldn't I have just said the fish was sick?

The splendid thing about having two children thirteen years apart (along with many splendid things like having a hero to worship who is also a built-in baby sitter) is that with the second all your lessons are learned, and you don't make the same mistake a second time. You make different ones.

Now that our built-in baby sitter, who has survived both his mother and the Army, is not here to cope with things that come up, like trying to persuade his little sister that there *is* a Santa Claus, I have to face the issues that arise in the daytime and trust to my own judgment. I hate to bother my husband at the office with things that seem trivial to a man. Only a woman knows how many little heartbreaks there are in a child's world. Which brings me to what happened the other day.

I went into my daughter's room a few minutes after she had left for school. My eye swept over the confusion of dolls, costumes, books, shoes, jigsaw puzzles, and the usual post-exit debris, and fastened on her aquarium. Floating on the surface was a goldfish—very dead. I hurried downstairs and said to the housekeeper, "Did Meg see her fish? It's dead."

"I don't think so," she said. "She would have said something—she went off to school very happy."

"I hate to have her upset," I said. "I wish I could keep her from finding out." How the years change one!

"Perfectly simple," said my remarkable housekeeper. "You simply match it."

"Match a goldfish?" I said.

"Oh, I've done it dozens of times for other children. You take it to the pet shop or five-and-ten and get one as close to it as you can find—I've never had a child find out yet."

I beamed at her, wrapped the fish in some tissue, and hurried to the five-and-ten. Rushing in the door, I bumped into an acquaintance.

"My," she said "you *are* in a hurry."

"Certainly am," I answered. "Got to match a goldfish before noon."

It's probably my imagination, but the few times I've seen her since, she seems to be avoiding me.

I approached the attendant of the aquarium. She looked kind and understanding. Her eyeglasses were so thick she rather looked as if she, too, were in an aquarium.

"May I help you?" she said.

I held out the fish. "I'd like to match this as closely as possible," I said, feeling rather foolish.

She peered nearsightedly down at the fish and recoiled. "What did you do to it?" she demanded accusingly.

"I didn't do anything to it," I answered. "It just died."

"Did you feed it?" she said dubiously.

"Of course we fed it," I answered.

"Fed it too much," she said.

"That may be," I answered, "but it's too late now to do anything but get another."

She held the fish to the light, like a swatch of material, and handed me the long-handled net. "I'll hold this up here," she said, placing her hand with the fish in it above the water. "You scoop 'em out till we find the right one."

Half an hour later, wet to my shoulders, I cried, "This one is almost perfect—no one but an expert would know. She is just a little girl—I think we can get away with it."

The attendant looked at me disapprovingly. "Too bad to deceive her," she said.

"Believe me," I answered, "it's better this way. I've learned from experience—"

She handed me the dead fish. "Do you want to take this with you?"

"Just file it, will you?" I said, laughing in a comradely fashion.

She had no spirit of fun. She dropped the old fish into a wastebasket and handed me the new one. "Need any grass, or feed, or a snail to keep the bowl clean?"

"Oh," I said, "I didn't know I needed a snail. If you think I'd better have one—"

"Probably died from a dirty bowl," she said reproachfully.

"Oh no," I said defensively, "we cleaned it all the time—put him in the basin so he could have a real swim, and gave his bowl a good scrubbing."

"Probably died from soap," she said.

I left feeling like a murderess.

I was leaning over the bowl in my daughter's room, watching the new fish circle around, and the new snail slither up the side, when I heard my daughter come in behind me. I jumped with as much guilt as if she had caught me in her piggy bank.

"Hi, sweetheart," I said, much too heartily. "I was just feeding your fish."

"Hi," she said, throwing her sweater on the bed. "No point in feeding him—he's dead."

The fish flashed around the bowl, and she ran over and peered in. She stared at him and then at me. It was a terrifying moment.

"Very funny," she said. "This morning he was dead, and now he's alive, and he has a spot on his side—he never had a spot."

There I was. "Well, you never can tell—" I laughed nervously—"what will happen in an aquarium."

She just gave me that look again.

I guess there is just no way to know the right thing to say to a child.

A WOMAN'S

CAREER

or

How Not

to Write a Book

THERE IS ALWAYS CONJECTURE about how a woman
can run a home and children while also being engaged
in some other work. How does she cope with a
woman's ordinary daily problems and her chosen
profession as well? How does she paint the picture?
Run the travel agency? Write the book? In short,
how does she get the job done?

The answer is perfectly simple. She doesn't. Or almost doesn't—somehow something gets done, but something has to give.

It is one subject on which I can speak with unques-
tioned authority. And, since I like to be of any help I

can, what I have done, in the knowledge that we can all learn from each other's experiences, is to jot down a few rules on How Not to Write a Book. I'll go slowly —you may wish to take notes.

Rule Number 1: Get married.

This is imperative in No-Booksmanship. By the time you are through doing all the important loving-wife things you should for your husband like picking up the clothes he has strewn for thirty feet across the floor, marinating the steak for him that he has decided to barbecue for dinner, picking up the film of those pictures he took on his last hunting trip, and watching over the laundering of the imported Italian silk shirts, your writing time has been cut down rather well.

Rule Number 2:

A. Have children.

B. See that that they attain a proper cultural background.

In this rule the age brackets of the children are inconsequential, because, regardless of age, their contribution to No Books is immeasurable.

Being recently emancipated from Michael's teenage parties, hi-fi jazz, and the removal of skin-diving equipment from the living-room floor, it occurred to me I might now be able to concentrate on my work. I was mistaken—our daughter Meg's school has an active P.T.A. that believes in a series of things called "Drives," "Festivals," and "Exhibits." If other schools are similar, you will find that by the time you have driven the cans to the can drive, the feast to the festival (and they love home-baked goodies—this means you), and the exhibit (generally alive—something like a white mouse or snake) to the exhibit, you have successfully shot a good portion of your working day.

But not all of it, because after school there is ballet class, where—if you are like me—you won't be able just to deliver your daughter, but have to stay and watch because the children are so enchanting, looking like little black sausages in their leotards, and it is so rewarding to see that *your* daughter is unmistakably the best in her class. Watching will take only about an hour and a half of your time and you could then go back to work, except that you are told your daughter is going to be in a performance given by the school next week, which naturally requires a costume. This again means you. My ballerina has in one year successively played an angel, a snowball, and an elephant, which I hope is no sign of the future for her. The construction of the costumes kept me happily away from the typewriter for days. But now she is making up for it, because she is taking piano lessons and has progressed to something called "The Cooing Dove." Any teacher, piano or otherwise, will tell you it is *your* interest and the sharing of *your* time which makes for progress. So I have found that I can sit with Meg and keep time to her music with my typewriter, assisting her as if it were a metronome. This way we share in our work. *Hers* is improving.

Rule Number 3: Keep up with your household repairs.

I'm not sure this shouldn't be Rule Number 1—it is so important. If you attend strictly to what should be done, "maintenance" can be absolutely guaranteed to keep you from ever writing a book (or painting a picture, or running a travel agency). It isn't so much the time you give to it; it's the time you give to the men who are giving their time to it.

You see, these men who come to your house (if they come to your house) are prepared to give you a good deal of their time. They can't fix it, whatever it is, but it does remind them of another one they couldn't fix—this lady had an even worse problem. An hour later you know all about the lady's problem but you don't know how yours is going to get fixed. It isn't—why don't you buy a good new water heater and not have to fool with this thing any longer?

There's another thing to remember about repairmen: It's not their fault. It's the one who was there before who didn't put it in right.

We have a forced-air heating system, which we had installed in the process of remodeling an old house. So it's our fault. We should have had a *good* firm do it. Anyway, this system is always sick. And the man who is supposed to make it well is terribly busy, except after hours—he can run over after dinner, but it is necessary to bring his little boy. His wife is at a club meeting. So, while he crawls about in the attic rapping things with a hammer, followed by my husband who doesn't think he's doing it right, I am privileged to take care of his little boy. The little boy wants to play with my little girl's dolls. She doesn't want him to play with her dolls. So I take the little boy into my study where I am trying to finish a chapter. He is quite good for a minute or two and there is no noise except the gentle pop pop pop of bubble gum.

Then he says, "Your daughter doesn't share."

"Hm?" I say.

"She's selfish."

"Who?"

"Your kid—she's awful."

Well, no one is going to say that about *my* little girl.

"She's not really, dear," I say patiently. "She doesn't like her doll's eyes pushed in—you wouldn't either, would you?"

"I haven't any dolls."

"Well, if you *had,* you wouldn't like their eyes pushed in, would you? They're sort of her children, you know."

"They're not children, they're plastic—"

"She likes to pretend, dear. Don't you ever pretend?"

"Nah. That's stoopid. She's stoopid."

"She is *not* stupid. She is an extremely bright little girl."

"You're stoopid."

The chapter isn't going well. I say patiently, "Why

don't you run in Meg's room and try to play nicely for just a few minutes? I'm sure your father is almost through."

He saunters slowly out, leaving the bubble gum in an exquisite little Dresden dish.

Back to the chapter. Then a shriek from my daughter's room, and she flies in, followed by the little boy. He was trying to push *her* eyes in.

It's best just to put the chapter aside and involve them in a nice game of parcheesi.

He cheats.

The other thing to remember about the men who fix things (or don't, as the case may be) is they are all writers. Boy, could they write a book! If only they had the time to fool around with it the way you do. Some day they're going to take the time off, and do it. Or maybe you'd like to do it. You could split the profits. Too bad you don't have the time, because the stories they could tell you. Wow! *Peyton Place* is nothing! As far as the refrigerator is concerned, you're going to keep right on having this trouble unless you put in a new unit—costs almost as much as a new machine—better turn it in. Call him, if you change your mind about the book. This is a *true* story—it'll really rock you back on your heels.

Rule Number 4: Answer the door.

When the doorbell rings it is not a check from your publisher or a notification that you have been awarded the Pulitzer Prize. If it *is* the mailman, it is because there's two cents due, and boy, do his feet hurt—he was saying to the postmaster just the other day if they didn't get carts, he was going to have to . . .

It is the county assessor, the Fuller Brush representative, some little girls selling Girl Scout cookies (and there's a mother with them, and she's thirsty—could she trouble you for a drink of water? What? Oh, they're all thirsty—come right in), or it is a salesman from a local cemetery wishing to sell you a plot—after all, one has life insurance; one should also be prepared for as little as five dollars a week to insure that one's final resting place be to one's liking; if one were to sign up this week, one would get in on the special bronze plaques, depicting the Book of Life—its leaves open, waiting for one's name to be inscribed—at no extra cost.

Try to get back to *your* book before it's too late. It is too late.

Rule Number 5: Open your mail.

You will find a series of surprises. Open the ones that are obviously bills first. This can depress you so that it is impossible to work at all. Then, because all the zip has gone, and you need to take your mind off yourself, open the rest of the mail.

You will find that everyone is worse off than you because of the number of requests for charity donations. You set them aside to discuss with your husband. Then you will find that every magazine printed in the United States is having a fantastic special subscription rate of eighty weeks for just pennies. The offers are too good to resist, so you sit down and fill out the cards. Later you find that your subscriptions to the same magazines have not nearly run out, so you get two of each of them every month, or week, and you and your husband can read them simultaneously with no discussion as to who gets it first—very relaxing.

Then you will have to send back that slip that is impossible to get unstuck from the cardboard cover of the Book Club wrapper if you don't want the book they're about to send you. You don't—you wanted the alternate—but you lose the slip, so you get the book anyway.

All this can take enough time so that it's too late to do anything but go to the market. It's no wonder you can never get any work done around here.

Rule Number 6: Discuss your work with your husband.

In the first place, it isn't really work. If you had to go to an office every day, and face the business world, you'd know what he goes through. You've never been in business, so you don't know. That's why you don't organize your time. You are a very good writer (or painter, or travel agent), and he's very proud of you, but if you are constantly going to tell him how hard it was to get any work done—don't do any work. It only creates a tax problem anyway. Just stay home and keep house like the rest of the girls. And by the way, why isn't there any starch in this collar?

MY LIFE

ON THE

CREAMED-CHICKEN CIRCUIT

or

How to Go

on a Ghost-to-Ghost

Hookup

Personally, I'd rather not write than be President. However, there is one thing to be said for writing a book—there must be. After the endless tortured hours alone with your typewriter, making two a crowd, battling through the periods where the head doesn't work at all, to the awful discovery that if you like it, there's something wrong with it, finally the most beautiful words in the world, which are not "I do" but "The End," can be written.

What a glorious moment, what a sense of accomplishment and well-being—well, look out!

One would think, that after months of harrowing labor, one would reap a harvest of peace and relaxation, wouldn't one? One would be out of one's ever-lovin' mind if one thought so. Because one is just beginning— one has to get out there and sell it, honey.

It seems that a new element has crept into American Literature: it is called Merchandising. The moment those two lovely hard covers, with your effort between them, appear, the hard sell begins. The publisher's earnest publicity staff urges the author into a series of television, radio, and women's club engagements because "Somebody-or-Other sold 300,000 copies by being on Jack Paar." They sort of sneak up on you, until before you know what hit you, there you are, ON THE AIR, with a Personality. Well, that's what seems to be happening, even when it sometimes isn't. I know it sounds confusing; I'll try to elucidate, but it probably won't be easy for either of us.

For my first radio interview I appeared on time at the proper station and asked politely for the Personality on whose show I was to appear. The attendant, without looking up from his copy of *Mad Comics,* muttered, "Fourth floor—Studio B."

I approached the attendant on the fourth floor who, without looking up from *The Racing Form,* said, "Who're you for?" It wasn't an election year, and I felt he had no right to ask, anyway.

"Pardon me?" I said.

"What show you want?" I mentioned the Personality, and he threw back his head and bellowed, "Mildruhd!"

People were running in and out of doors and huddling in tight little conferences in the hall. A young woman moved away from one of the groups. The attendant said, "She's for you."

The young woman looked me up and down as if she felt I couldn't possibly be. She had crisp blond curls and matching manners. Her pale gabardine suit sported in its breast pocket a brilliant flowered handkerchief ironed into rigid, fan-shaped folds sharp enough to cut any nose bold enough to blow on it. The handkerchief was skewered into the pocket by a blue glass pin shaped like a daisy. Someone must have given it to her because it matched her eyes, which also looked like blue glass.

"You have an appointment?" she said dubiously.

I introduced myself, said the Personality was expecting me for an interview.

"You the one that makes hats out of palm fronds or the baby sitter for the chimpanzee?"

Disclaiming both interesting occupations, mine seemed anticlimactic—I confessed to it.

She riffled through some papers and said, "Oh yes, I've got you—follow me. We'll have to hurry—the studio is scheduled."

She clicked off down the hall with such alacrity that

I had to run to keep up with her. After winding around a succession of corridors, she said, "Here we are," and we entered a large padded cell.

It was all dun color with quilted walls. One little table, two chairs, and a microphone stood alone in the middle of the otherwise empty room. A man in a control booth stared through glass at us like fish in a bowl.

"Sit there," snapped Mildred.

"Get a level on her," croaked a voice from the gold-fish bowl.

"Say something," said Mildred.

"One two three four," I said. "Good morning. Now is the time for all good men to—"

"Tell her to get it up," the goldfish said.

"Up," said Mildred, as if she were about to follow it with "Hup two three!"

"By the way," I said, making conversation, "when is Mr. Reilly expected?" That wasn't the Personality's name, but it will have to do.

Mildred looked at me in surprise. "Oh, he's not coming," she said. "He never does."

"What do you mean?" I cried. "How can he interview me if he isn't here?"

"Too loud," came the voice of the goldfish.

"Down," said Mildred, as if she were going to follow it with "Bowser."

Mildred handed me a typewritten sheet of paper. "Obviously you're new to this," she said. "On this paper there are a series of questions which I will read. You answer them. Later they wipe my voice out of it, and Mr. Reilly records the questions when he gets around to it—he can knock off six or eight of you people at one time that way."

"You mean to say," I said, stunned, "that the answers come before the questions, and the interviewer isn't even here—well, I'll be d—"

"Cut!" cried the goldfish.

"Watch it!" snapped Mildred. "No profanity."

Her eyes were on the wall where a red light flashed on. "We're on," she said. "Now Mr. Reilly will start by introducing you and then will say 'How do you do'—say 'How do you do.'"

"How do you do," I said.

"Now he'll do a commercial," said Mildred. "Then he'll say something like, 'May I call you Cynthia?'"

I nodded.

"So then you say something like it's okay, if you can call him by *his* first name—it's Al. Maybe you laugh it up a little."

"Ho ho ho," I chortled to the empty studio. "Yes, if I may call you Al."

"His first question: Why did you write the book?"

"Because somebody paid me to."

"Are you married?"

"Yes."

"He'll have some jokes here—he always does about marriage—laugh."

"Ho ho ho."

"Any children?"

"Yes, two."

"How old?"

"Six and nineteen."

"He'll make a joke about that gap in between—laugh."

"Hee hee hee."

"Now he'll do another commercial."

It went on like this for fifteen minutes. "Okay," said Mildred. "That's enough. Say 'goodbye.'"

"No time," came the voice of the goldfish. "Got to run another one."

The red light went out.

"May I go now?" I said.

"Why not?" Mildred answered, gathering up her papers.

"Dig you later," said the goldfish.

He waved a fin through the glass at me.

"Thank you," I said.

Mildred and I walked to the door. I put out my hand, and she grasped it as if it were a hockey stick, simultaneously scanning her wrist watch. She shook her head. "It's a rat race."

I wasn't sure what she meant, so I said, "You ain't just whistling Dixie," because I have never known what that meant either, but it seemed to fit in.

Later by sheer accident, I heard the broadcast. It didn't go too badly, until the end when the invisible Mr. Reilly said, "It's been a pleasure having you on our show. We know the book is going to be a smash—good-bye, Mrs. Lindsay." Absolutely dead air. I hope Mr. Reilly understood that I was cut off at the controls, that I really wanted to say goodbye. And that it had been such fun not meeting him.

Having conquered radio, I was next flung, live, into a series of ladies' luncheons, where panels of authors spoke and, after lunch, autographed copies of their books for the ladies. Each luncheon lecture held its individual surprises and enchantments, but certain aspects of all of them were absolutely uniform. It was *always* creamed chicken, and the lunches were *always* expensive for me. Not because I had to pay, but because I felt so sorry for the authors whose books the ladies weren't buying to be autographed that *I* bought them to be autographed. The books that go well with the ladies are the ones that the authors have carefully told them he hopes won't offend them because they are, well—outspoken, as in the bedroom scene, because that wasn't the author's intention; he just wanted to show *life,* and sometimes *life* is *raw.*

I have a huge collection of wholesome autographed books in my library.

By the time I had knocked off a dozen lunches, all the ham had come out, and instead of decently suffering, I began to enjoy myself. I merrily said yes to television and found myself in strange company at strange hours.

My first TV interview was with a man who came on

at eleven-thirty at night and proudly stated that just about anybody could be on his show. That meant me. When I arrived at the studio, in the chill California night, everything was apparently in a complete state of chaos. People were charging about dragging lights; men with earphones carrying microphones leaped over cables, and prop men hauled furniture about. I inquired for the Personality and a man seated at a desk under a barrage of lights was pointed out to me. I walked over to him and introduced myself. "Hi, honey," he said, holding up my book. "This any good?"

"You haven't read it?"

"Never do," he replied. "I used to be a literary agent —could always sell something better if I hadn't read it—more objective, so to speak."

He looked up at the wall clock. "Say, you'd better get to make-up—you're on third, between the bathing beauties and the singing dog."

"Make-up?" I said.

"Sure—have to—you'd wash right out without it— no eyes."

"Heaven forfend," I said and, my head spinning, followed his directions to the make-up department.

There were four chairs lined up in front of the mirror. They were occupied respectively by two young girls in bathing suits, an old man, and a dog of dubious ancestry. Six other girls in bathing suits were busily applying body make-up to themselves under the interested gaze of a mild-looking man whose made-up yellow face looked incongruous with his conservative business suit.

"Hi," said the make-up man when I walked in.

"Hi," I said.

"Get to you in a minute, honey—got a couple ahead of you."

We all sort of smiled at each other awkwardly. The man in the business suit said, "I'm Clark LeRoy—Malevolent Savings and Loan (it sounded like). I'm going to talk on the growth of loan companies in California."

We shook hands and I introduced myself.

"What's your racket?" he said.

"I'm a writer," I answered.

The old man in the make-up chair said, "I once had a friend who was a writer. Had some kind of record—two hundred words on the head of a pin. Can't beat that, I'll bet you."

"I'll bet not," I said. "I find it hard to get that many on a page. What's your racket?"

"Him," he said, pointing to the dog whose deportment was admirable. He hadn't moved, just sat staring quietly at himself in the mirror. "He sings."

One of the young girls giggled. "You're kidding," she said. "With lyrics?"

The old man looked lovingly at the dog. "This is a big break for us. I hope something comes of it. He's never had a real break, have you, Titan?"

Titan twitched an ear and looked limpidly at his master.

"He's darling," I said. "I can't wait to hear him sing."

"Well," said the old man, "you won't have to. We're always glad to oblige."

He took a small whistle out of his pocket. "All right, boy—'Yankee Doodle'!" He blew the whistle, and Titan put his head back and in a piercing tremolo let loose with a reasonably accurate canine rendition of the song. We all applauded enthusiastically, until someone outside yelled "Quiet!"

"That was just wonderful, Titan," I said, patting him. He smiled and thumped his scraggly tail. "He's certainly not going to get made-up, is he?" I asked his master.

"Not much," he said. "Just a little kohl around the eyes—he washes out."

"My trouble exactly," I said.

"Okay," said a voice from the door, "you're all on, let's go."

The make-up man said, "But I haven't done her—"

The man at the door looked at me and said, "Well, slap something on quick. We'll put her on later." My new associates left me in a pack.

By the time the make-up man had given me eyes, and a lovely, sensuous mouth bordering on the Ubangi, I was late for my spot on the show. But it all worked out fine, because the Personality let me judge the bathing-beauty contest instead of talking about my book, which was much more fun.

In the course of the months of odd-hour television

shows on which I performed like a trained seal, I met many interesting and stimulating associates. None, admittedly, that I took to quite like Titan, but the experience was rewarding nonetheless. I shared the limelight with a collection of African masks, a director of freeway traffic patterns, a young woman who had been arrested for soliciting but thought better of it and became an evangelist, a real witch doctor, a collection of teen-age jive experts who had not read my book but did want me to join the dance (this didn't work out well). I finished the season in what was almost a starring role. The show went on the air at seven o'clock in the morning, with a notable cast: a jellied omelet, a trained rabbit, and me. The rabbit and I were each a smash. The omelet came out beautifully, and the rabbit and I ate it.

THE CONFESSIONS

OF A PACK RAT

or

How to

Pack a Gondola

No! Not in Greenland at five in the morning and thirty below zero—no, no, no! You're going to drive me crazy!"

My husband and I, and a hundred or so other passengers, had put down in Greenland on a flight over the Pole, my first lap on my first trip to Europe. And he was objecting because I wanted to do a little shopping!

Being my first trip, I had been delirious at the prospect. My husband, having lived in Europe, was naturally superior about the whole thing. "Everything," he said, "depends upon intelligent packing. Take half as many clothes and twice as much money as you think you'll need—the first rule of the smart traveler."

So I had packed twice as many clothes as I ever needed, and they were all the wrong ones, anyway, and I figured he could worry about the money, and he did. Then I filled the bags with little treated cloths for washing when there was no water, little treated papers for drying when there were no towels, medicines for every known human ailment including beriberi, and numerous plastic containers which leaked. I was ready.

My husband said, "I've never seen such carrying on—you've been at it for a week. I can pack for anywhere in the world in ten minutes' time."

An hour before we were to leave he telephoned and said, "Throw a couple of suits, some shirts, underwear, and my razor in a bag for me, will you?"

In a frenzy I packed his three bags, placing his shirts —carefully wrapped in tissue paper—alone in one, so they wouldn't muss.

Five minutes before it was time to leave for the airport, my husband sauntered in as if there were no need for speed. "I thought you said *you* could pack for anywhere in the world in ten minutes—"

"Relax," he said with infuriating calm. "I can see it now. You're going to be completely hysterical—having overpacked to begin with. You're going to shop endlessly, and then you are going to lose your luggage . . ."

So there we were in Greenland, the black icy night around us, and the warm cozy airport with that charming shop. It wasn't ten minutes before I had a beautiful piece of amber, a darling little Eskimo doll, four fuzzy white toy polar bears, and three seals made from real skins. After all, Christmas was only a month away and every child I knew would adore them.

"But it's the first day, and we'll be gone three weeks, and you are already overweight—" My husband's voice had taken on a desperate quality.

Then I showed him my marvelous bag. I had bought it with the avowed purpose of outwitting the airlines. It looked like a purse—an absolutely enormous purse—but had the capacity of a suitcase. "They'll never weigh it, so there is no overweight problem, and I'll never ask you to carry it—a deal?" I said, stuffing the fur animals into it.

He looked martyred. "I only hope you don't leave it somewhere," he said. "You know how you're always forgetting things—and I refuse to be responsible for that zoo."

In Copenhagen I was so overwhelmed by the beauty of the fairy-tale city that I kept gasping all the way from the airport to the hotel.

"No matter how excited you are," my husband said, when we had reached our hotel room, "always keep your luggage in mind. Now before we start out on the town, how many pieces of luggage do you have?"

"Four," I answered promptly, "counting my junk bag."

"Good girl," he said encouragingly. "Making, with mine, six in all."

"Seven," I said.

"Honey," he said, "you never could count, but you have four and I have two—that's six, no matter how you slice it."

"You *had* three," I said. "Count them."

He looked puzzled and counted. "No, just two—see for yourself."

"Where are your shirts?"

"My shirts? Why—oh no!"

It was the perfect start for the perfect trip. I was intact. *He* had lost a suitcase. It was rather expensive getting the suitcase from the airport but worth it.

Copenhagen, a shopper's paradise, contributed largely to my junk bag: new things, old things—but no light things. A few we sent home. Two items for which I still hold customs declarations never arrived. They are a *gron kunde* and a *kladesbiosh*. I'm sure they're lovely. I wish someone would tell me what they are.

In London we were fortunate in being loaned an exquisite little flat in a mews off Piccadilly which, aside from being beautifully furnished with rare antiques, was beautifully furnished with a rare butler. After welcoming us as if we were visiting royalty, he said, "May I unpack you, Madame?"

Everything was done impeccably. Pretty soon my husband's side of the room looked like a well-kept monk's cell, mine like a stall in the Flea Market.

The lovely butler was marvelous, never raised his eyebrows. "Madame is a collector?" he said.

"Madame certainly is," said my husband, his eye roaming the clutter. "It's almost impossible to stop Madame when she gets rolling."

"Does Madame know of the Portobello Road?" said the butler.

"Unfortunately Madame does," said my husband. "She's aiming for there in the morning."

"If Madame needs anyone to accompany her to bargain, I should be pleased to offer my services," said this paragon.

I was in a state bordering on euphoria. My husband didn't have to go with me and be patient, and I would have someone to haggle in shillings.

That night we were dressing for the theater and my husband called from the bathtub where he was lolling, "Get me a shirt, will you, darling?"

I searched the beautifully laid-out drawers and called the butler. "Where did you put Mr. Lindsay's shirts?"

With no change of expression he said, "Mr. Lindsay has no shirts, Madame."

My husband called, "Oh yes, a whole bag full—the little pigskin bag."

"There was no little pigskin bag, sir," the butler called back.

I started to giggle. My husband started to gurgle. Then from under the water came a faint "Oh no."

It was even more expensive getting the bag back this time. We had to hire a car to go to the airport for it. The marvelous butler unpacked the bag, gently smoothing the contents. "You know, Madame," he said, "I *did* think it odd for a moment when I unpacked you—your husband had no shirts, and you had four bears, three seals, a brass doorknob, a stone tortoise, a snuffbox, an ivory cat, and a clay owl, but then I said to myself, 'After all, they *are* Americans.' "

The marvelous butler was even more marvelous on the Portobello Road. No longer gentle, he bargained and haggled and shook his umbrella at the stall keepers, and we returned laden with treasures at bargain prices.

Into the junk bag went some real Egyptian scarabs from a real tomb, a bronze dog-head umbrella handle, a brass bird with garnet eyes, some handsome ormolu heads, a dragon door knocker, and odd small objects both heavy and breakable. The Staffordshire lions wouldn't fit and had to be sent.

The butler was just as much of a junk hound as I. The day we were leaving he presented me with an old plate featuring a picture of a child squeezing a large dog very tightly and bearing the title "Dear Friends." I have never been so touched.

Paris and the Flea Market were pretty hard on the junk bag. The yellow Moroccan-leather footstools wouldn't fit, so my husband had to incorporate them into his luggage, which he did while graciously mumbling something about not minding if he *did* lose that one.

Rome was the worst because everything was either bronze or alabaster. The bag, along with its other treasures, already held some pieces of agate from the gardens of Windsor Castle—combined with the chunks of marble from the floor of the Coliseum. But I smilingly carried on, my shoulder now completely out of its socket.

In Rome I bid my husband and my son, who had flown with us from Paris, goodbye and took off across Italy alone on the Orient Express.

Alone and unobserved, I scoured Florence, and the bag began to sag at the seams. But Venice was what tore it. The bag, and the situation. By this time the weight of the junk bag had become so much a part of me that even without it I walked with a slight list to starboard.

In the morning I sauntered beside the canals, wandered through the squares, drinking in the beauty of the city, resisting the impulse to take anything more home with me. Then, at the end of the day, just as I was on my way back to the hotel, I saw him.

He was in the window of an antique shop and I knew, heavy or not, expensive or not, I had to have him. He was a brass sea horse about a foot high. The bit in his mouth had brass reins attached. He was gay, spirited; he was Venice. He was mine. The lovely creature had been the decoration for the bow of a gondola at one time, the dealer told me; there was still some wood from the bow to prove it. He gave me an old piece of blanket to wrap around my new treasure.

Like a raccoon scurrying to wash his food, I hurried back to the hotel and scrubbed my latest acquisition.

The sea horse needed polish, but I hadn't any, so I just washed him, and his blanket, thoroughly.

He was the first refusal. He simply wouldn't pack. Not in the junk bag. Not in any bag—he was too heavy.

For the rest of my journey we were inseparable: I carried him, like a mother her first-born, wrapped carefully in his awful blanket through Milan, Nice, Monte Carlo, New York, and back to California.

My husband and daughter met me at the plane. As I stepped off, carrying my junk bag over my shoulder and my swaddled treasure tenderly in my arms, my husband stared at the bundle. "Do you have something to tell me?" he said.

"Is it a sister?" said my daughter.

"No, it's a sea horse," I answered.

Neither of them looked pleased.

The sea horse became integrated into the house immediately. I had a black ebony stand made for him, and now he gallops gaily on the table in the front hall.

SEE

WHAT THE BOYS

IN THE BACK YARD

WILL HAVE

or

How to

Inundate Togetherness

Are you ready to take the plunge?" cried the advertisement. "It's not too late, if you start *now,* for you to know by this summer the happiness of a swimming pool in your own back yard—the greatest way of bringing a family closer—the family that plays together, stays together."

Well, there was no problem about being close to our children, as well as everybody else's children. Our children like us; all those other children like us too. Might be a very good idea to put in a pool—it would get them out of the house.

So, with enormous excitement, we started clipping ads, pictures of pools, pool landscaping, garden furniture. Then we started consulting the pool builders themselves. (That is, after we consulted the bank about the loan. The bank said it was all right if we wanted to go to all that trouble and mess, when it looked like maybe the freeway was going to go right through our house anyway. "They can always put a bridge over it," said my husband weakly—he didn't really share my wild enthusiasm for the project.)

We didn't go into it foolishly or impulsively. We read brochures, viewed documentary films on pool building, and heeded warnings by each concern on the pitfalls of dealing with rival concerns. Ultimately we simply tossed a coin. As they were all the *best* we couldn't go wrong. When the great day of contract signing arrived, we looked at the contract (not very carefully, it developed), and I glowed with pride at our newly established status symbol. Under our names the contract stated: "Hereinafter referred to as owners."

"What a moment!" I said. "Look at that!"

My husband said, "I am looking at it—it scares the hell out of me."

Then the wheels began to turn. Inspectors from the city arrived, dug their toes in the dirt, kicked the driveway, checked our gas system, our electric system, our access for bulldozers. They were all not enough, too much, too soft, too hard, or too far away.

The pool salesman arrived for his final appointment to try to dissuade me from my choice of a shape for the pool. I had said very clearly, and right from the start, "I know this is radical, but I want a pool-shaped pool— no kidneys, no livers, no heart shapes—I want a pool shaped like a pool."

The salesman simply said, "We will give you, of course, whatever you want, but *nobody* has them that shape any more."

"I do," I said. "We have enormous space with which to work. At the end of the garden are those six magnificent Italian cypresses. I want the pool to start from here and lead straight up to the cypresses. We'll have fountains in this end. You'll be able to see through them—it will make a wonderful vista. The effect will be almost Roman."

Anyway, the salesman, as I was saying, was there for his farewell visit. The job of the salesman is to promise you everything, and the job of the engineers is to see that you don't get it. There is no liaison between these pool people. They hate, and devote themselves to the undoing of, each other; the only person undone is you. They share only one quality: they require a great deal of servicing. Everybody connected with pool installment requires constant servicing . . . that's your job. Their backs hurt; they are hot; they are thirsty, and it's all your fault.

At the end of our final consultation the salesman rose to go, shook my hand, and said, "Well, so be it—it's your pool—but you've wrecked its resale value."

"We aren't going to sell it—we're going to swim in it," I said. "Of course, just having had a gall-bladder operation," I added, "we could make it gall-bladder-shaped and just set my one perfect stone in the middle of it."

"Wouldn't lend itself to the formality of the garden—too irregular," he said seriously. "You haven't got a spot of bourbon on you, have you? I'm whipped."

I poured him a drink. He belted it down and said, "Thanks—I have to blow. Do me a favor, will you? Here's my telephone number—call my wife and tell her I'll be late. I have one more appointment . . . so long—good luck." He vanished forever.

I called his wife and said he had another appointment.

"I'll bet," she said. "And who might you be?"

"Just a client," I said.

"Ha!" she snapped, and hung up.

We had been promised that work would start immediately after the signing of the contracts and that we would be notified so that we would be prepared. There was complete silence for a week, then we woke one morning with all hell breaking loose. I have never heard (or *had* never heard) a more horrendous noise—it got worse later. Bulldozers careened up the driveway, felling trees in their wake; steam shovels followed,

snorting and stretching their long necks out like pre-
historic monsters. A small army of men carrying picks
and shovels followed the monsters. We ran downstairs,
greeted the men with enthusiasm, and their fearless
leader said, "That the spot?" He pointed to the staked-
off area. We nodded, and he yelled, "All right! Let
her go!"

The monsters roared into action. Bushes flew into
the air; dirt piled up, and before you could say, "Don't
go near the water," there was a gigantic gaping hole in
the garden.

"I feel as if we should have at least broken a bottle
of champagne over the bulldozer," I said.

"Not a bad idea," said the leader. "You got any beer?
It's hot out here and, boy, am I hung over."

My husband went for the beer, and the workmen
who were standing around watching the bulldozer
chew up the earth allowed as how they could use
one too.

Over the whining roar of machinery the leader said,
"You checked your main water and sewer lines before
you laid out this location, didn't you?"

"No," I answered. "Nobody even mentioned them—
the salesman said we could have the pool wherever we
wanted it."

"Somebody ought to pop those guys," he said, frown-
ing.

My husband returned with a trayful of beer. The men
thanked him and said not to bother—they'd just help
themselves in the future. My husband looked at me. I

just shrugged, and I didn't mention the pipelines—
he was on his way to work and I didn't want to worry
him.

Our family plumber dropped in to view the proceed-
ings. We had been through a lot together and were on
a very friendly basis. "Hit anything yet?" he said
cheerily.

"Please," I said, "don't mention it."

"You will," he said. "I just stopped by to tell you
I was going to Las Vegas for a few days and you
couldn't reach me, but my new partner's on call—he'll
come right away. Wow, it's hot—you got a coke?"

I gave the plumber his coke. He thanked me and
started for Las Vegas with, "I'll be seeing you. Boy, are
you in for it—I wouldn't be in your shoes!"

I went upstairs to put on the shoes he wouldn't be in,
and boy, was he right! I looked out the window just
as—with the roar and whoosh of an oil well coming in,
but with dissimilar financial gain—a geyser of water
rose thirty feet in the air, past the window, and splayed
back over the surrounding territory. I raced downstairs
and gasped to the leader, "The main water line?"

"Right," he said.

"What are you going to do?" I said, standing under
the shower of Old Faithful.

"Nothing we *can* do," he replied. "Call your plumber
—he'll shut off the line and lay in an emergency one for
you. You don't have another beer, do you?"

"If you will just wait until I call the plumber—" I ran
into the house, called the plumber's number, and a voice

answered, "Mrs. Lindsay? I figured it would be about now—Harry told me. I'll be right over."

In a few minutes a large white Cadillac pulled into the driveway. A smoothly dressed man in black alpaca sweater, matching slacks, and silk shirt stepped out. I went out the back door and said, "Yes?"

"Mrs. Lindsay?" he said. "I'm the plumber."

"You *are?*" I said, then recovered and took him to see the geyser.

He viewed it with no expression, then looked past it at the hole for the pool. "This as far as you're going? How long is it going to be?"

"Thirty-six feet," I answered.

"Mine's fifty. Why did you put in such a small one?"

"Well, it seemed large until just now," I said. "What are you going to do about the broken pipe?"

"I'll send someone," he said.

"*Send* someone! Can't you *do* something?"

"I am a plumbing contractor, Mrs. Lindsay, *not* a workman. I will have someone here within the hour. The water will be turned off, which will leave you with no water at all. Then we'll lay in an emergency pipeline as a temporary measure. . . ."

As we talked, I found my gaze drawn to an orange tree which, being slightly out of the fallout area, was one of the few that hadn't had to go to make way for the pool. As I watched the tree, it slowly sank into the ground, as if being pulled under by evil trolls.

"Oh, my God!" I said.

"What's the matter?" said the plumber.

"That orange tree is sinking into the ground right in front of my eyes!"

"It must be because the tree is over the sewer line and they've hit that too," he said cheerfully. "By the way, I wonder if you have a little something cold?"

Ultimately the plumber's workers repaired the water line in and the sewage line out, laying the latter at a slant that brings everything back *into* the house instead of *out* of the house.

Three weeks, several thousand dollars in plumbing bills, fourteen cases of beer, and numberless near nervous breakdowns later, a gigantic steel basket reposed in the pool hole, and the inspectors said, "O.K. to pour." The pool was ready to be lined with gunite. Gunite is concrete applied pneumatically under great pressure by huge machines that make the world's most terrible noise. The process is pretty unnerving to watch, and rough on the men, but a good cold beer always helps.

When the guniters dragged away, blessed quiet prevailed, and the garden with its gaping hole, its piles of dirt, and its splattering of empty beer cans was deserted, except for the steam shovel standing by, its jaws gaping. The quiet was broken by the arrival of a convoy of dump trucks. The steam shovel, alerted, smacked its lips with a clang and started chomping at the piles of dirt, then, getting its fill, spit it into the waiting trucks. I hurried to the truck foreman. "You were told, weren't you, that I want a truckload of the dirt left here for landscaping?"

"Who said so?" he shouted above the noise.

"I did," I said. "I told the engineer."

"Between those damned engineers and the salesman —they'll drive us nuts yet. We've got a placement for this—most of it's good topsoil."

"I know," I said. "That's why I want it—and it's *mine*."

"I don't know," he said. "This is part of the deal— it costs us plenty to run these trucks, you know."

"That really isn't my problem—just leave a truck of topsoil." I turned, went into the house, and didn't even offer him a beer—there comes a time when somebody *has* to be the boss.

He called after me, "You got any iced tea? It's hot out here."

"Right away," I answered weakly.

I made him the tea and took it to him. "I'm leaving for a while—I'll be back later," I said. "Just leave the topsoil."

Mistress of the situation, I left and did not return until the end of the day. The pool area was completely leveled and there was no topsoil—anywhere.

I am seldom hysterical, but the following morning the pool company received a call from me that might be so described.

"Take it easy, lady—don't get yourself in an uproar. We've got a lot of jobs going. We'll bring you some dirt—"

"But I don't want just any dirt. I want *my* dirt, my lovely topsoil."

"Lady," he said patiently, "dirt's dirt. Hold on to your hat—we'll get some to you today."

I left the house with no faith in his promise.

I returned to my home in the afternoon and, driving up our cracked driveway, came face to face with a mountain of dirt. Right in the middle of the driveway. Three truckloads of pale, claylike, adobe dirt. Dirt is *not* dirt; adobe is impossible—nothing will grow in it. I ran into the house, called the pool company, and the man said, "Well, you couldn't expect us to haul it into the back yard, could you?"

"I didn't want my beautiful topsoil taken in the first place—"

"Oh, lady," he said, "relax. Fill it with peat moss, fertilizer, blood meal, and leaf mold—it'll be fine—"

"My dirt *was* filled with peat moss, fertilizer, blood meal, and leaf mold, and this dirt is *not* fine on the driveway—you can't even walk by it, let alone drive by—"

"Lady," he said, "we said we'd dump it—it's dumped."

That night it rained, a heavy, California, flood-type rain. The adobe mountain melted, flowed over the driveway, into the driveway next door, over our front lawn, and into the street—and there was still a large portion of the mountain left. The fine from the Street Department was only fifty dollars. They said we were lucky to get away with that.

The pool was now ready to be plastered, but the

plasterers couldn't get their equipment past the mountain in the driveway. "Call us," they said cheerily, "when you've moved this away." By this time, having survived a series of setbacks, I didn't even wince. I didn't call my husband—poor man had enough trouble. I didn't call the pool company, having long since learned that lesson. I just called a trucking company and paid to have the dirt carted away.

When the earth-moving problem was settled, we called the pool company and said, "O.K. to plaster." The crew arrived bright and early and along with their equipment brought a novelty, their *own* beer. All they wanted me to do was to keep it in the refrigerator. My heart went out to them at once—their own beer, imagine!

When I put the beer on ice for them, I just didn't notice how *much* beer they had brought. I watched the fascinating process of plastering for a little while—the incredible speed with which the men worked, the deftness with which they sloshed it on, smoothed it off. Then I had to leave for an appointment. When I returned, the telephone was ringing, and over the sound of it was an uproarious chorus of hollow voices interrupted by hiccuping emanating from the bottom of the pool.

"Hi," said my husband's voice on the telephone.

"Hi," I said. "Hold on just a second, will you?"

I went out and looked over the edge of the pool and returned to the telephone. "Hi—"

"Just checking in," he said. "How are the plasterers?"

"Plastered," I answered. "And I fear for them—it's a blazing white shell with the sun beating down into it, and they're all dead drunk. *Now* who do you think I should call?"

"Alcoholics Anonymous," he said. "It's the only way we'll ever get the job done."

Somehow the men finished the job, plastering themselves into the corner and up the steps, sweating and hiccuping. "It's beautiful," I said.

"Thanksh," said the head plasterer. "Losha tension in this work—gotta work againsh time—you happen to have any beer?"

"Yes," I said, "but why don't you just get into your truck in the shade, and I'll bring it to you there—then you'll be heading for home."

"Shasha great idea," he answered. "Come on, boys—'headin' for the lash roundup—'" he sang as his men weaved after him.

The voice of the plasterer high on his truck rose in song as I hurried to the house, "Oh, bury me not on the lone prairie . . ." The voice stopped as I returned to the truck and handed them their beer and checks.

"Thanksh," said the plasterer. "Now at exactly nine o'clock tonight shtart filling it."

"The pool?" I said. "So soon? But how?"

"Jush you turn the little ole garen hoshe into it—it'll fill. When it gets up to the tile line—*shtop*. Then call the company . . . sho long."

"Sho long," I said, and he roared down the driveway in reverse.

When my husband came home, we started looking at our watches every minute until the magic moment arrived. At seven he wanted to fill it; at eight he insisted on filling it, and we had a fight, and I won, and promptly at nine we turned the hose into the pool. All night we were lulled by the gurgle of water running into our very own pool. We had no idea how many other things were running into our very own pool. Our cat and dog, who had been playing games chasing each other up and down the sides of the empty pool, had invited some friends over, and they ran up and down the sides of the almost empty pool, leaving these darling little paw prints on the white plaster.

The next morning I looked out the window and said to my husband, "How about that? It's really there—a pool, a real pool full of real water. I just may go down and get right into it."

"Why don't you?" he said. "It's about time you got some pleasure out of it."

I slipped into a suit and walked up to the edge of the pool and then turned around and walked right away. The whole pool was full of worms. I was standing staring in horror when the pool-maintenance man arrived. I pointed to the pool, transfixed. "Don't worry about it," he said. "Happens all the time—the worms come when you put the new lawn food on. Sure is hot— you got a glass of ice water?"

You see, what happens, apparently, is that the worms are crazy about this lawn food, eat it, and then go swimming too soon after lunch, and you know what that does. Serves them right.

At long last, after learning the why and wherefore of pool ownership, to deal with "suction areas, anti-vortex action, insurance policies, 'round the clock protection,' mechanical alarms," the pool lay, clean, clear, wormless, and inviting, a thing to be proud of, a symbol of having made it in life. On the deck of the pool lay a series of presents from friends. So many presents that, when the presents were in the pool, there was no room for the people: a wet rocker with pneumatic buoyancy, a boat, a horse, a swan, a raft, a large bubble, a life buoy, a plastic seal, a pool bench for sitting half-submerged, and a basketball game. When my husband arrived home from work, I said, "This is it, tonight's the night —I'm going in!"

"Good girl!" he said. "I'll not only join you, but you go ahead, get into your suit, and I'll bring you a bottle of champagne."

"I don't believe it," I said. "Somebody is going to bring *me* a drink in my back yard?"

I rushed to change, and in a few minutes we stood beside the sparkling waters, sparkling glasses in our hands. "It's been a long hard fight, Ma," said my husband, "but we made it. To the pool!"

"To the pool!" I said, took a long sip, dived in, hit the bottom, and broke my nose.

THE

GOOSE ROUTE

or

How to Say,

"Audience—Go Home"

W HAT IS REFERRED TO as the vast video audience, lying
on its TV pillows, munching its partially thawed TV
dinners followed by its crispy crunchy TV snacks, little
knows, and little cares about, the degree of human sacri-
fice made on the altar of its entertainment medium.

It is a magic medium. The magic is that it ever gets
on the air at all.

My association with the business started with selling
the television rights to a book I had written. The hope
was that after making a pilot film it would be bought
for a series. The book had been a simple one, a childhood autobiography of mine, dealing primarily with
my relationship with my mother, a lady who was, to

understate it, a nonconformist. I wrote a television script based on the book which, I hoped and felt, maintained something of my mother's character. There was considerable enthusiasm about the script: it was "fresh," "different," a "whole new approach to situation comedy."

So there I was with what I thought of as a completed script—everybody loved it; there couldn't be much to do to it. The star suggested for the part loved it; the agent involved loved it; but the studio which bought it didn't love the star who loved it and said briefly, "Get lost." The star was justifiably hurt, having been a part of discussions and conferences, and having not only begun to think of herself as the star but also the writer.

This last, by the way, is the commonest occupational disease of television production: Everybody thinks he wrote it, unless it's bad. Then *you* did, honey.

After the elimination of one star we started on a long series of others. I wasn't consulted about whether the star might be suitable in any way to the part; I was just told I could tailor Mother to the star. Tailoring Mother to life had never worked out very well. I hoped, now that she was gone, that immortalizing her might be an easier job. She would have taken a dim view of some of the selections for her immortality. We went through six stars via multiple submissions and at one time reached an interesting impasse when two said yes simultaneously. They decided— (A word about "They": They are people "up front" who make decisions. But They must not be held responsible for them, because if it doesn't come out right, They didn't do it. You did. After having told you to, and the result is a fiasco, the reason it is is because They told you *not* to in the first place. Don't try to understand it; just accept it. It's the rule.)

Anyway, They decided on the star They thought had greater drawing power. The chosen star then had a fight with the producer and quit, and the other star, mad at being turned down once, wasn't going to touch it again, not with a ten-foot pole.

Meanwhile, back at the typewriter, I was writing another pilot for another star, a young and lovely one, whose talents for some years had been upstaged by a dog in another series. Neither I, nor the producer, could "lick" the story, so it was decided that the star should be Mother.

So I started happily all over again with a star I liked and a script she and everyone involved liked. And then I learned my first important lesson: If anybody likes it, and if it is bought because it is different, the first thing you do is listen to all the things that a succession of people don't like, then you must try to make it exactly like everything else *because* it's different.

So we had another story conference: "Honey, you don't get the message—this dame is a Kook, but she's got to be a lovable Kook, otherwise the public won't accept her." "Mother was not," I said, "a Kook. She was a true primitive, and everyone loved her." "Divorce yourself from your mother, honey. This is another kind of dame. We think we'll change her into an aunt, anyway—she'll be more acceptable—the mass media mind will not accept anything but complete goodness as its image of motherhood. Besides, this way we get the jump on Auntie Mame."

"Auntie Mame has had the jump on us for some years," I said. "Let's not fight her now—I think she's got *us* licked."

I won the battle of Mother, changed the sex of two leading characters, and rewrote one male villain who had to be lovable though villainous, because "otherwise it's not comedic," and one female villain who had to have a Pekingese written in to show she was a society woman.

Then we started the most important job to date: casting.

With the aid of casting directories and casting directors, we had little trouble finding good people until we came to a leading character who wasn't a person; he was a goose. In the original script and in real life his name was Sydney and he belonged to an elderly vaudevillian who came to live in Mother's house. Sydney had a little hat with a feather on it, which he wore proudly and would not remove. The part didn't call for a great deal of dramatic ability; Sydney just had to wear his hat, follow his master around, and be found by some children while he was swimming happily in the bathtub.

I'm sure that getting the horses for Ben-Hur's chariot caused no more trouble than trying to cast Sydney. I received daily bulletins from the nice people who knew I cared. "Honey, we've found a goose, but the damn thing has no talent and hates hats." Then in rapid succession, "Let me toss this at you—a turkey that wears a dress suit—" No one was going to toss a turkey in or out of a dress suit at me. "Well, I guess I agree with you—I doubt if the public would accept him as a sympathetic character." Then, "We've got a penguin— what do you think?" "Crazy about penguins," I said. Then the next day, "Scratch the penguin in your thinking, girl. He's molting—looks like hell. But don't worry —we've got a call in for a duck. I'll get back to you."

I was adjusting my thinking to the duck when the last casting call came through. "Are you ready for this one? The director's been interviewing a chimpanzee— now don't say anything. I know it's strictly from left field, but he's crazy about this chimp. It wears a little suit and does absolutely anything, including smoking cigarettes—it borrowed the director's lighter, lit its own cigarette, and returned the lighter—I think that's what got the director. What do you say?" "Uncle," I said.

The first day of shooting was both exciting and sentimental for me. The star, who was my friend, wore my mother's bracelets. The cast had an understanding of her character, and there was a feeling that she was about.

I'm convinced she was, and knew they didn't know

the edge of the tub. Sam put out his hand, scooped up some bubbles, ate them, and smacked his lips. Then the trainer urged him gently over the side. Sam went along with it until he realized where he was, and then he started to scream. Still screaming, he leaped from the tub, splaying a barrage of bubbles over everything, ran wildly into the living-room part of the set, flung himself, sobbing, on a couch, and pulled a Spanish shawl over his head. "Cut," said the director.

Sam's trainer picked up a whip and moved after him. Sam, no longer earth-bound, leaped onto the mantelpiece, to the top of a light, to the catwalks, and dropped onto the neck of the second cameraman who had earlier established himself as Sam's friend. The darling man said, "There, there, Sam—don't cry," and he walked him up and down, Sam's arms around his neck, like a baby, Sam snuffling and mumbling in his ear. "I know, I know," comforted his friend. "Show business is hell."

Sam's trainer approached him, and Sam, secure in his new friendship, gave the trainer the raspberry. The trainer removed him from the cameraman's arms, saying, "You and I are going to have a little talk." He led him away from the scene. Sam, no fool, followed him with his head down. He knew he was in for it.

They returned a few minutes later, Sam docile and bubbleless, and the trainer said, "We're ready."

The trainer led Sam to the tub, lifted him in, and backed out of the scene. Sam experimented with the bubbles, ate a few, turned a few faucets (doubtless his capsule training), then found a bar of soap, and proceeded to eat it very slowly and with great relish.

Still wearing his top hat with the feather flying, Sam picked up a bath brush and carefully scrubbed himself with it. The children entered, reacted in surprise, called in another actor who reacted in surprise, and Sam continued his performance. When all the actors had come and gone, he turned his face to the door, did a splendid raspberry, and finding that this created more bubbles, he delightedly sat there blowing them until the director cried, "Cut! Sam, you're a great man!" and we all applauded. Sam joined in, and his trainer led him away for a change and some sunflower seeds.

An important studio figure (even higher than They; he was almost He) had come down to view the day's shooting. He turned to me and said, "I've put a hold on that chimp—he may very well be the star of the show."

"Afraid you can't do that," I said. "He's going into capsule next month—he belongs to the United States Government."

"The hell with the government," he said. "He's under contract to us."

I thought this a little subversive—a man should be willing to give at least one chimp for his country. However, it was not for me to judge. Besides, there was no time; we were up to the drowning scene. The star, looking lovely in a brief bathing suit, approached the edge of the tank where she was going to rescue the little boy, because the chimp had come to warn her of the danger.

Sam and his trainer walked up. The director said, "All right, sweetheart, this is where you read your sundial speech. Sam listens to you, then warns you that the kid is in the pool. You climb the tree, dive in, and rescue him—right?"

The star stroked Sam's head and he looked up at her limpidly.

"All right, sweetheart, action," said the director.

The star picked up a sundial and read from its surface: "Fill ye every hour with kindness to all God's creatures." As she read her line Sam affectionately licked all the body make-up off her arm. She put the sundial down and read her next line: "All God's creatures—that certainly includes you, Sam." She leaned over him and he reached up and studiously pinched her on the bosom.

"Ow!" she screamed.

"Cut!" said the director, roaring with laughter.

"At least that dog never did *that!*" said the star. "We'll be banned in Boston!"

The trainer led Sam away, and they had another little talk.

They returned, and with some difficulty and replacement of body make-up the scene was successfully completed, everybody rubbed down, and the wet and uncomplaining star taken away to have her hair fixed for the final and very important dinner scene.

Dinner scenes are notoriously difficult to direct, because everyone sits around talking and not doing anything. But not this one. Once Sam's diverse talents were recognized, he set the table, ate his dinner, beat on the table with a spoon, did a series of raspberries, then smoked a cigarette, blew out the director's borrowed lighter, then tried to pocket it. The little boy reached for it, and Sam bit him. Hard. The child's mother sobbed, "I knew it—I should never have let him work with that damn monkey. He got bit in a Tarzan once— he's never gotten over it."

"Probably smelled the kid's fear," said the trainer. "Come on, Sam, we're going to have a little talk."

The child back from the hospital, his bandaged hand under a napkin, Sam, chastened, back in his seat, smoking away, the allegedly gay, happy dinner scene was finally successfully shot with the trainer sitting under the camera, a whip in one hand, a gun in the other, aiming at what appeared to be *all* the actors, including Sam.

Then the ever-patient star said, "Now, at long last, I get to play a scene, I, me, alone, all by myself." The star, among her other talents, had a fine singing voice, and it was decided in the middle of the shooting that it might be nice to let her use it. "Open up the show," it was called. "Give it another dimension." So, after the dinner scene, we moved into the living-room set to open up the show, and then Sam closed it. It seems that the trainer had forgotten to mention that Sam also played the piano. What better? He could accompany the star. She was doing a little something from *The Mikado,* which just happened to be in Sam's repertoire.

It was then decided that everybody might as well be in the scene. The entire cast sang, danced, put on hats, Spanish shawls; the star sang, and Sam banged away wildly on the piano.

"O.K. Cut." The director laughed. "Now we'll come in to a close shot of Sam at the piano and then we'll fade out."

"I was under the impression that this was my pilot," said the star, patience running out just slightly, "not Sam's—someone go get me a collie."

It was *then* decided that she was right, it would be better, after all, to fade out on the star, because two big sponsors were interested in the show because she was in it, and she was not only good but also wholesome, which was good for both soup and insurance, which they were selling.

We shot the last scene with the star getting an award for bravery, for rescuing the little boy. She turned to Sam and said, "The award belongs to him who earned it," put it around Sam's neck, and we faded out on the medal—an impartial choice.

After the final shot we all said affectionate goodbyes, had a drink together (Sam and the children had cokes), and said we'd see each other *very* soon because we were going to sell the show.

Then I went, a few days later, to see the rough cut

of the show. It was indescribable. I staggered from the projection room into the glaring California sun.

A week later I was told to go to work on rewrites. I worked, interspersed with story conferences with a variety of people whose job was to throw out what had been written on the direction of the people in the other story conferences. *They* seldom appeared, and He just sent directives which, when complied with, were rejected on the basis that that wasn't what He said. I was beginning to be at the end of my rope, came to the studio one morning, having worked straight through an entire weekend on revisions, and said, "As far as I'm concerned, tell God, my Co-pilot, that this is it—I've had it."

"I know you have, honey," said one of my friends who knew I cared. "He's got two new writers on it."

I was too stunned to do anything except pick up my papers and walk out so They wouldn't have the satisfaction of seeing me crying. Aside from the ethics of hiring other writers without first consulting me, the fact that what was my script, my book, my life, was being turned over to someone else was so shattering that I cried until I got it out of my system, then threw things at walls pretending they were They, but primarily He.

I should have gone to the Writers Guild with my complaint but I didn't go to the Writers Guild; the new writers did, demanding an arbitration to give them sole teleplay credit for the pilot. So I read their script, called the Guild, and said, "Let them have it, I don't want my name on it."

"Then you won't get the residuals—you can lose quite a bit of money."

"All right," I said. "I'll bring over all eleven of my scripts, months of notes, and a couple of hundred pages of rewrites, and you make up your minds."

The Guild Arbitration Committee awarded me sole teleplay credit, a major victory had it allowed me to use a pseudonym. The same day I received a call from the star. "Thought you ought to know we're finished with the retakes. There's a new ending—you know, where I'm supposed to give Sam the medal, saying, 'It belongs to the one who earned it'? Well, now the mayor comes in—"

"What mayor?" I said.

"Oh, honey, don't ask questions—there's a mayor, believe me. So now the end is, I say, 'The medal belongs to the one who earned it,' but the mayor says, 'No, no, you keep yours. Mrs. Robinson and Mr. Plummer have a special—'"

"Robinson? Plummer?" I said. "Who are they?"

"Stop interrupting—we add new characters and lines every day. Anyway, the mayor says, 'There's a special award for Sam,' and we cut to a close shot of a little girl chimp wearing a dress, and they kiss—are you listening?"

"I'm trying not to," I said.

"Well, brace yourself—there's more."

"There can't be."

"Well, that *was* the end, but then they decided that somewhere along the line I *was* the star, so now we fade out on a close shot of me turning to the character that is supposed to be the owner of the chimp, and as we watch them embrace, I say, 'Don't think you've lost a son—you've gained a daughter.' You're not saying anything—"

"What can I say, dear, after I say, I was just awarded sole teleplay credit?"

There was a pause. Then she said, "Make two stiff martinis—I'll be right over. You shouldn't be alone at a time like this."

The star and I have heard very little of the fate of the pilot. First it was so bad it was going on a one shot on an anthology show. Then we heard that it was so good that it had been removed from the anthology show and was being saved for next season.

One hopes that pilots, like wine, improve with aging.

Several good things have come from the ordeal, however. Like any baptism of fire which people share, I have gained a few very good friends and a clear-cut, no hanky-panky enemy. Some of the actors were so good in the show that they have received considerable work because of it, including Sam, when available from his labors for his uncle of the same name. He is apparently so good at the capsule controls that he may really go into orbit. It's a very comforting thought to me in my time of sorrow—Sam in the sky, rocketing overhead, smoking away between raspberries and nibbles of sunflower seeds, playing the piano in the cosmos—an interstellar star of first magnitude. I'd just like to see the Russians match that.

I hope he occasionally gives a thought to me, down here, earth-bound, going the Goose Route.

WHERE THERE'S

A WILL

or

How to Plan Your Life—I Mean Death

WHEN I HAD LIVED alone with my small son, I had taken my responsibilities to the other human with great seriousness. I told myself, constantly, that a woman alone bringing up a child was not a good thing, that I must not allow him to be tied to my apron strings, that I must shake him out of the nest, that I must not overprotect him. So I overprotected him right up to the eventuality of my death.

There has never been, I am sure, a more elaborate will than mine. It included instructions for his free choice of friends to look after him, my wishes for schools, things I wanted him to do, things I wanted him not to do, each member with individual qualifications to fill his specific needs.

After several pages devoted to his lifetime care, I disposed of my personal effects to the many kind friends who were going to oversee the rearing of my son. There were a few family pieces to be given to his wife, on his marriage. With a proviso, however, that if she didn't like garnets, Grandmother's necklace was to be put away for their first daughter, my grandchild. Michael was four years old at the time.

Having taken care of Michael's future, spiritually, educationally, and materially, my next concern was for our pets. Never having been without a number of them, I worried deeply. Small ones Michael could keep, but large ones seemed an imposition on friends who would be caring for him.

I had a good friend who loved animals in general, but our dogs in particular, so the last page of my voluminous will read, "Any and all dogs to Barbara Diamond."

Then I relaxed and proceeded to live my life with a clear conscience.

When my husband and I were married, we threw out the old will after he had laughed hysterically at it for some time. Then we made duplicate new ones, saying I got everything, or he got everything, depending upon who was first gathered to his forefathers. The will was one paragraph long. We stuck it in the safety deposit box and forgot about it.

Then the opportunity for my first trip to Europe arose, and my husband commented, "It's really extraordinary how much territory you can cover when you're flying."

"Flying!" I said. "But we can't fly together!"

Having two children, we felt we had no right to risk the possibility of their losing us both in case of accident.

"Oh, I think now we can," said my husband. "If we don't, half the fun of the trip is gone."

"It wouldn't be any fun, anyway, if we were worried about the children—" I said sadly, seeing my beautiful trip slipping through my fingers.

"May I remind you," my husband said, "that our children are now six and nineteen, that the nineteen-year-old is a man, that he is in the Army, that he adores his sister, and that he is a very capable and sensible human being."

"And he could take care of her!" I said. "I never thought of it. And anyone he marries would love her— he wouldn't marry her otherwise!"

"Precisely," said my husband. "I'm much richer dead than alive, so that's no worry—and the house will be theirs."

"But what if the Army won't let him out? Who's going to take care of her?"

"Willie, of course," said my husband.

Willie is our beloved housekeeper, a woman of enormous strength of character and of conscience.

I said, "I know Willie would stay and take care of Meg, but it's a terrible responsibility—I hate to ask her."

"We could set up a sort of advisory board of friends on whom she could always call—"

"Of course! But this a pretty large house—I wouldn't want to ask her to take care of it *and* Meg."

"We could provide for additional help."

"I just want to know that she will always stay with her. With her as mother and Michael as father, she'd be as well off as with us."

"Better," said my husband.

"Well," I said, "I guess everything depends on Willie and Mike—shall I call her in now for a family conference?"

"By all means—unless you'd rather pick out a family plot first, so that we can be prepared."

"This," I said, "is not a joking matter."

Willie was marvelous. "Why, yes, I'll certainly do it," she said. "However, I'm not nearly as young as I used to be."

"We're going to arrange for additional help," I said. "It's just that we want you to be the one to actually care for her."

"I assume," she said, "you will be putting this in writing? I have a friend who had the unfortunate experience of being left in charge on the request of the parents, and the executors let her go."

"It won't be necessary to put anything in writing," my husband said. "Michael will be in charge, and he loves you as much as Meg does."

"Well, I don't know," I said. "The Army might not release him immediately. I think we'd better make a formal will."

"Oh, don't be ridiculous—all right, do be ridiculous

if it makes you feel better. I want you to really enjoy the trip—call the lawyer in the morning."

In the morning I explained the situation to the lawyer who said, "We can just draw up a letter. Make three copies. You write everything you want done. File one copy with me, one with your housekeeper, and put one in your safety deposit box."

"Are you sure," I said, "nothing can go wrong? They couldn't take Meg away from her brother even though he's not yet of age?"

"Not with the number of friends you've named to act as executors—they know what you want done."

"But what about Willie?"

"*They* know you want her. *She* knows you want her. Michael will know when you tell him that you want her, and I assume he will want her himself."

"Oh yes, he's mad about her—and her Toll House cookies."

"Now," said our lawyer, "if you'll forgive me—I have an appointment. Your son, by the way, should be very proud that you put so much faith in his ability to raise a family."

"He'll do a great job," I said happily.

Then I called most of the friends listed as helpers in case of emergency. They were willing, nay, proud, to be named.

Then, harking back to my first will, I went to work on my new masterpiece. It wasn't easy. Some of the friends in the former will have moved away . . . and the needs are different now, I kept telling myself. After all, Michael is a grown man with a wife and a child—no, he isn't, for heaven's sake—well, he will be—and what if Meg and Mike's wife-to-be want the same pieces of jewelry? Of course if Meg were older we could just divide them. However, the material things are not important; the emotional needs are what count. Fortunately with Willie and Mike and Mike's wife (what a marvelous girl!) and the board of loving friends, Meg will probably be fine. Everyone is to remember that despite her sensitivity she needs a firm hand otherwise she takes the bit in her teeth—gentle, but firm—for her own sake. Personal discipline is so important in later life.

Everything we had, of course, belonged to the children, except for a provision for a pension for Willie and some personal things. The animals Michael would naturally take splendid care of, so that was no problem, except that he was definitely to help Willie with Mo, the Siamese cat, whom she really hated but fed anyway. He would please personally cope with Mo.

The religious training was to be Michael's choice also. He could decide what was best for his sister. She was, at the moment, she said, "an Epispeterian."

Meg was to live with Michael, his wife when he got one, and Willie until of age, then they could all decide what was the next best move. I did leave them that choice. It seemed a little soon to pick a husband for her. Michael could do that.

All three copies of the document were notarized and filed. I took a deep breath and, completely carefree, started to pack.

After an emotional farewell to Meg and a tight hug, and "Thank you for everything" to Willie, off we flew over the Pole to Copenhagen, where we cabled Michael, who was stationed in France: CAN YOU GET LEAVE STOP MEET US IN LONDON STOP WE WILL ARRANGE TICKET STOP NOTIFY US LONDON ADDRESS. We signed it formally *Mother* and *Father,* in case his superior officer read it.

On our arrival in London, there was a cable waiting for us: HAVE LEAVE HAVE TICKET STOP ARRIVE ONE O'CLOCK STOP LOVE MIKE.

On the way to the airport to meet Mike, my husband said, "Please, just don't start off with the will routine. Let's let the boy enjoy himself before you explain his new responsibilities to him."

"I thought he'd consider it an honor—"

"He will, but do you mind if we just have a little fun first before you bury us?"

"I shall say nothing until you, in your wisdom, deem it the proper time," I answered huffily.

At the airport, as all six feet three of Mike descended from the plane, my husband and I looked at each other with tears in our eyes. It had been almost two years since we had seen him. He was a man. A grown, responsible human being. Not to mention handsome. I gulped with pride, and we all enveloped each other.

London was glorious. We saw every sight, visited

with old friends, went to the theater, the ballet, drove to the country, and my husband's and my main pleasure was in watching the way Mike handled himself in any place, in any situation. He was a really fine fellow, and we no longer had anything to worry about.

Then the three of us were sitting across from each other at a table, sipping champagne and toasting our reunion.

"Mike," I said, "here's to you."

"You bet," said my husband. "By the way, I'm afraid with all the excitement we neglected to tell you of your new responsibility in life—"

"I'll tell it," I said. "You see, we could never fly together because of the responsibility of you children, but we suddenly realized that you were a man, and that whoever you married would love Meg as much as we do, and that Willie would stay on to keep house for you, so we've left you in charge of everything—you should be terribly flattered."

My son looked at me. "Mom," he said, "I'm both flattered and touched, but—"

"You won't have to have all the responsibility," I went on. "We named a board of Anne and Charlie, Fran and Victor, Phyllis and Alan, Patsy and Jules, Marg and Michael—"

"But, Mom—" Mike said.

"And they'll handle things until the Army releases you."

"Mom—" Mike said.

"Willie has a list of doctors' names in case of emergency."

"Mother!"

"You can do what you please with all the stuff—*that's* not important. What is is that you will be with Meg now, your wife—"

"My *wife?*"

"Well, you know—when you have one—she'll love her, too—won't she?"

"Mom, everybody loves her—but—"

"Don't interrupt," I said. "Anyway, we thought you'd like to know how deeply we respect your ability to take care of everything, if anything should happen to us—"

"Mother, just shut up for *one* second and *look* out the window!"

I did.

Then we all looked at each other. Then my husband and my son began to laugh. Then they began to laugh harder.

The table at which we all three were sitting was between our seats on the maiden flight of the first jet plane out of London for Paris.